CW01594729

SPINE-CHILLERS

MIDNIGHT MADNESS

Edited by Emily Wilson

First published in Great Britain in 2016 by:
YoungWriters
Remus House
Coltsfoot Drive
Peterborough
PE2 9BF
Telephone: 01733 890066
Website: www.youngwriters.co.uk

Book Design by Ashley Janson

SB ISBN 978-1-78624-111-5

Printed and bound in the UK by BookPrintingUK
Website: www.bookprintinguk.com

FOREWORD

Enter, Reader, if you dare...

For as long as there have been stories there have been ghost stories. Writers have been trying scare their readers for centuries using just the power of their imagination. For Young Writers' latest competition Spine-Chillers we asked students to come up with their own spooky tales, but with the tricky twist of using just 100 words!

They rose to the challenge magnificently and this resulting collection of haunting tales will certainly give you the creeps! From friendly ghosts and Halloween adventures to the gruesome and macabre, the young writers in this anthology showcase their creative writing talents.

Here at Young Writers our aim is to encourage creativity and to inspire a love of the written word, so it's great to get such an amazing response, with some absolutely fantastic stories. We will now choose the top 5 authors across the competition, who will each win a Kindle Fire.

I'd like to congratulate all the young authors in Spine-Chillers - *Midnight Madness* - I hope this inspires them to continue with their creative writing. And who knows, maybe we'll be seeing their names alongside Stephen King on the best seller lists in the future...

Jenni Bannister

Editorial Manager

CONTENTS

STOVER SCHOOL, NEWTON ABBOT

THE HARRODIAN SCHOOL, LONDON

TETTENHALL COLLEGE, WOLVERHAMPTON

THE MINI SAGAS

Solitude

Walking for days, I came across the town. Forgotten buildings rotted in ranks in the sand. I stopped in front of the old saloon, hoping something was left to drink. A door slammed. *Just the wind,* I told myself. But there was no wind. Walking into the bar, the air chilled. *Just the wind,* I told myself. But there was no wind. I heard a whisper in my ear, not quite deciphering it. 'There is something behind me,' said my subconscious, but I didn't turn yet. *Just the wind,* I told myself. But there was no wind at all.

Bryce Jersing (15)
Abingdon School, Abingdon

The 12:01

12am. Dan shivers, alone on the deserted station bench. Can't sleep. His dad, the old stationmaster, dead and he can't forget his presence. A jolt! A rush of howling air. A train! A real train creeps to a macabre stop. The train door opens by itself. He slides one foot onto the train. A chill, a whistling breeze. Nobody. Carriage by carriage. *Strange,* he thinks. *Who'd drive at this hour?* He's close now to the driver's door. The door squeals open. Nobody - but a chilling presence. Smoke. Marlboro cigarettes. Dad's. *Slam!* The door again. Jjjj! The lights have gone.

Ben Ffrench (15)
Abingdon School, Abingdon

Sanguis Tristis

I stare at my reflection, the candle flickers out. My mind takes a deep breath: preparing for the psychological onslaught. I struggle and stagger, I fall, slipping into the mirror. I stumble back up, the candle dancing, re-lit, dancing in the draught. Light failing to penetrate the looking glass. My reflection is lying on the ground, steaming blood dripping from my serrated wrists. It puddles on the tiles, beading along the cracks. My hair piles around my face, smothering my features. The shadows around me gather, smoothing the edges of the white sink, filling it. My depression has won.

Silas Gill (15)
Abingdon School, Abingdon

Sticks And Stones

In the dark shack, the boy stumbled. Thirty seconds... a minute, they wouldn't know the difference. Laughing, he sprinted from the shack to the place where his friends had dared him. They were gone. His laughter bounced off the cold, steep quarry walls and he could hear the distant clamour of his friends growing fainter. He moved towards it. His laugh grew louder again: deeper, hollower, sharper; it became a cackle. It grew unbearable and he ran. He tripped and fell down the pile. He lay there for a second then he heard a boot lightly crunch next to him.

Louis Brosnan (15)
Abingdon School, Abingdon

Phobia

6:30am, Sydney. I could feel the sweat trickling down my spine as I ran my morning run over the dunes and onto the beach. My bare feet burning on the golden sand as the music pumped into my ears. The dark, haunting clouds chasing behind me as I jogged my way back home. I was unlocking the door when I felt a stinging, striking pain in my leg. Time passed through the day and my eyes were heavy. I switched my lamp off and tried to fall asleep.
I woke up the next morning and the wound had grown...

Abrielle Johnston (14)
Ashford School, Ashford

The Toymaker's Doll

The newest addition to my shop is Dolly. When I dragged her up from the cellar, I noticed the back of her head was damaged. A new wig took care of that. I applied blusher to her pale skin and painted a smile on her face. I stitched her mouth shut and tried to curl her lips into a smile but they were too stiff. I stepped back to admire my masterpiece. She was perfect. All I needed was a high-collared shift to hide where I'd slit her throat.

Anwen Iris Williams (13)
Ashford School, Ashford

Suicide

Sergeant Higgins surveyed the scene, trying to pursue the matter. He could be sure for one thing that the man was dead. Higgins couldn't find an explanation for this matter. The victim was smartly dressed with a bow tie. No one reported any gunshots but there were holes with blood spilling out. He came to the conclusion that the unidentified man committed suicide.
His ghost stayed with Sergeant Higgins, for he was the one who found him.
One fateful night Higgins was found hanged in the forest on the very spot that the man died.

Millie Rimmer (13)
Ashford School, Ashford

Shadows In The Graveyard

They had played in this graveyard before, but tonight seemed different. The moonlight danced behind the clouds and the temperature dropped suddenly. Both girls saw shadows move towards the church, and heard the door bang shut, then creak open. They stared at the church nervously. The old roof sagged wearily, showing years of decay. The heavy wooden doors gently blew outwards towards them, like the arms of an old friend beckoning them onward. The girls crept towards the church doorway. Silently they opened the door and ventured inside only to see the vicar staring terrified at something behind them...

Rebecca Jones (11)
Bury Grammar School for Girls, Bury

The Corner Of My Eye

I look out of the corner of my eye, she is standing there, a sinister look on her face. She drifts towards me. I don't dare look. I'm lying in my bed, adrenaline crawling up my body. The lights flicker supernaturally. I can hear the roaring thunder outside, the lightning joining its tantrum. I hear screaming in the house. I hold my breath. I can taste blood in my mouth from where she knocked out my teeth. Suddenly, all is quiet. I look out of the corner of my eye... she is holding my sister by the neck - dead!

Layla Gardner (11)
Bury Grammar School for Girls, Bury

The Voice From Beyond

It was a dark, frosty night. Lightning lit up the sky like a firework display. Lisa lay in bed, unable to sleep so she crept downstairs to watch a film. She tiptoed downstairs. She couldn't turn the TV on. Suddenly the radio started. It was saying, 'I am coming back now.' Lisa could feel sweat dribbling down her face.
Again the croaky high-pitched voice started, 'I am on your road.' Just then she looked at the door. She saw the handle slowly turn left and then it was there. It came through the door. It was her brattish sister, Bethany.

Abigail Whiting (11)
Bury Grammar School for Girls, Bury

My Last Breath

An eerie shadow owned the street. The darkness blinding, the silence deafening. The graves stood around like guard dogs and the buried bodies slept. A piercing scream broke the silence. For some unearthly reason, the church seemed to lure me in, towards the danger. I crept away from the safety of my room. Through the door I tiptoed, until an uncertain moaning noise rang out. It was coming from behind the darkened altar. Nearer and nearer towards the danger I stumbled, as the noise grew louder and louder. Suddenly a hand grasped my back, and I took my last breath...

Chloe Alice Parkinson (12)
Bury Grammar School for Girls, Bury

The Boy In The Mask

Emma and Jess were excited because they were getting ready to go to a Halloween party. But not just any Halloween party, Shaun's party - the most popular boy in school. They arrived at the party and something was wrong, they could feel it. They didn't care, they were too excited. Suddenly a tall man walked in wearing a mask. No one knew who he was or where he came from. As the night went on people were disappearing but no one was going home. Then it was just the two of them. A voice appeared behind them, 'It's your turn now!'

Eve Chadwick (11)
Bury Grammar School for Girls, Bury

Something, But What?

I was only going on a relaxing midnight walk, I wasn't doing anything wrong. I was striding through the graveyard, rapidly trying to find my mother's grave. I only wanted to put some red roses onto it... Meandering around every grave I heard a noise, I thought it was a bird so I just kept on searching. The noise was getting closer and before I could turn around, I felt a hand on my shoulder. It wasn't a familiar hand... As soon as the hand touched me I heard a loud screech and nothing else. Nothing else ever again.

Emily Chadwick (11)
Bury Grammar School for Girls, Bury

The Devil, My Devil

I was in bed on the gloomy eve of Friday 13th, too scared to go out, too scared to stay in. Out of the corner of my eye I saw a shadow, a big and terrible shadow. There was a tapping, an uncontrollable, sinister tapping attacking my ears. It sounded like a creature was scuttling across my newly varnished wooden floor. I didn't know what to do... to stay or to go? As it came closer I could see horns, much like the Devil's. Red eyes flickered against the shimmering moonlight, was it really the Devil? No, just the cat!

Hana Khan (11)
Bury Grammar School for Girls, Bury

The Two Brothers

Up in the tree, I watch them, the brothers. Laughing and joking in the deserted street. They don't know what's coming. They seem young, but he'll be angry if I don't do it. He's always angry... I swoop in. The street lamp goes out, I grab the older one. The street lamp comes back to life in a second but by then I've done the deed.
The younger brother shouts worriedly, 'Liam! Where are you?'
'Look up,' I hiss in the darkness.
The younger brother looks up. He screams. His brother, drenched in blood, hangs by his neck.

Harriet Nicholson
Bury Grammar School for Girls, Bury

The House

Joe left me alone. All alone. Where was I to go? All there was were trees... and a house. I walked up the eerie path leading to the grey, dull, abandoned house. Was it really abandoned though? It might have been an illusion, but when I opened the door, smoke rose from the chimney... I walked through the door. I heard people whispering my name, beckoning me with their voices. Pictures on the walls started moving, I heard glass smashing upstairs, then I saw someone walking down the stairs. Who was it? Oh my, no, it can't be, it's... me!

Alexandra Anne Joan Quarrell (11)
Bury Grammar School for Girls, Bury

Regret It

It was a cold and stormy night when - *bang!* - she was there! Her bony wrinkly skin made me feel sick. I watched her as she stepped into the room; I had chills up my spine. As I awoke I heard a voice say, 'You're gonna regret it.'
I was sure I had heard that before. In my dream I had seen a little boy cut across the throat by his mother and it was her.
'You're gonna regret it!'
He said, 'Mommy, you scared me.' And that was all I remembered.

Chiedza Chavunduka
Bury Grammar School for Girls, Bury

Tunnels Of The Dead

I shuddered as me, Michelle, Amber and Dan walked through the eerie bone hallways of the catacombs.
'This was a bad idea,' Dan said through his chattering teeth.
I completely agreed with him.
'There's no turning back now!' yelled Michelle.
We pushed on, determined to find an exit. Suddenly a piercing shriek struck the air.
'A corpse grabbed my leg!' Amber said, stammering.
Dan held her hand was we carried on. Our claustrophobia kicked in. Almost simultaneously our flashlights began to flicker. Then it happened. We saw nothing, but we heard a voice like no other, it whispered, 'Lights out.'

Phoebe Booth (11)
Bury Grammar School for Girls, Bury

The Voice Of My Daughter

Annabelle suddenly stumbled upon the derelict church that had been hidden by trees. She felt compelled to find out what was behind the decrepit wooden doors. No sooner had she entered, she was overcome with fear as she heard hushed voices muttering from all corners of the church. The base of her spine tingled as a cold blast of air brushed past her arm. She wanted to leave but fear rooted her to the spot and she felt a trickle of cold sweat on her forehead. The voices had changed and now they were whispering her name over and over.

Olivia McCoy
Bury Grammar School for Girls, Bury

The Spooky House

It was a bright and lovely day when I was wandering through the woods. All of a sudden I saw something.
What was it?
It was an abandoned house.
That night I went back!
I went up to the house. As I got nearer, I got more and more frightened. Then, to make things worse, I saw a ghostly figure. When I went into the spooky house, I couldn't see anyone at all. All I could see were normal things, like a television, wooden table, desk, chair and a white tiled kitchen.
Then someone or something said, 'Is anyone there?'

Lauren Bradley-Holt (11)
Bury Grammar School for Girls, Bury

Three Girls And A Knife

One Halloween night three best friends, Kelly, Shirley and Annie had a sleepover at Shirley's lake house. The three friends went up to the attic for some sleeping bags and they found three Chucky dolls in a circle with a knife in the middle. There was one Chucky doll for each friend, with named necklaces around them. They pulled the string. Annie's said, 'You will die.'
The same for Kelly but Shirley's said, '*You* will be the murderer.'
Once they were dead Shirley smiled as the red blood poured from her friends' hearts and giggled, 'I never liked them anyway.'

Evie Stainer (11)
Bury Grammar School for Girls, Bury

Music From Heaven

Lucy was walking home from school when she saw something that wasn't usually there. It was a church with a ginormous bell, and a long skinny tower. She slowly tiptoed in and left the door ajar for her own reassurance. She was planning on coming out when... she heard the door slam. The organ started playing and she could hear people singing. A gust of wind flew past her; she shivered, and then tried not to scream. The organ started moving closer to her, she ran towards the door; the singing got louder, louder. Will she ever get out...?

Amber Lily Greensmith (11)
Bury Grammar School for Girls, Bury

Dark, Bleak, Blackness

Through cracks I see what can only be described as the horror of your worst nightmares; glowing red eyes, scar-covered skin, blood running from every pore. Terrified, I sit motionless, transfixed by fear. My heartbeat is becoming more rapid by the second. I try to control my breathing but the creature begins to lean in towards me. In a rush of fear I run, but I'm not fast enough. As I glance over my shoulder I see it grabbing for me, hands clasped around my neck. Loss of breath, burning throat, organs imploding - then dark, bleak, blackness.

Jo Daisy Maria Barker (15)
Canterbury Steiner School, Canterbury

Swallowed By The Hangers

Cackles booming from the clouds, for they laugh at me. The rain beats me to the ground. As the lightning strikes light the sky the trees lean over, pushing me into the centre of the path. For I did not wish to get snared. The leaves crawl towards me so I speed up. The thunder booms again. I shiver furiously. I start running and slip. I hit the hard ground, my vision is blurred. Something tightens around my ankle. I'm lifted into the trees where I'm slapped before being trapped in its belly. The trees are evil. Beware forever everyone!

Jak Taylor (15)
Canterbury Steiner School, Canterbury

The Shadow Walker

'Mum please read me this story.'
'OK... A family were slaughtered by their own shadows. The shadow walker watches you all the time; he controls your shadows and your dreams. If you're reading this book you are probably dead.' She slams the book and says, 'That's enough.' She goes off to wash the dishes.
All of a sudden a scream comes from upstairs, she runs up and looks at the boy with a rope around his neck, looking soulless. She sprints for the phone but she trips down the stairs and perishes. Watch out, he is behind you, he's here!

Josh Vincent Fiallos-Delpy (14)
Canterbury Steiner School, Canterbury

The Cursed Book

There was a family who lived in the woods. This family read a cursed book on Halloween. But before they read the book there was a strike of lightning. The family was scared. The book was called 'The Headless Man'. It said that people had disappeared if they didn't finish the book. They read it. They didn't finish it though because they thought curses weren't real.
By the next day they had disappeared. Their friends have not seen them since Halloween. There has been word that the family still haunt the house in the woods.

Zander O'Donovan (16)
Canterbury Steiner School, Canterbury

Pop! Goes The Weasel!

The soft chimes of the bells were a celebration to her ears. She was in. The toys sat on the shelves with creepy smirks but she didn't seem to notice. She ambled closer to the jack-in-the-box in the middle of the room, it wore a demonic, red-stained smile. The soft background music started to get louder.
'All around the mulberry bush.'
The crank slowly turned.
'The monkey chased the weasel.'
It turned faster.
'The monkey thought 'twas all in good fun.'
The clown snapped its head up and muttered, 'Pop goes the weasel!'

Morola Oyefesobi (13)
Eastbourne College, Eastbourne

The Full Moon

The wind was fierce, howling through the trees. I stood alone in the darkness awaiting his arrival. The leaves fluttered. I flinched. Branches snapped. I froze. This was it. Slowly, I turned and there he stood, tall and handsome, but something had changed. 'Sorry I'm late,' he smirked, as he leant against the sodden tree. He moved closer, his strides large but slow. My breathing stopped but my heart beat faster. His eyes were black and clouded, his teeth were long and sharp. He pressed a kiss to my shoulder. 'I'm sorry,' he whispered as his fangs pierced my neck.

Olivia Sykes (15)
Eastbourne College, Eastbourne

Behind The Warehouse

I crept through the abandoned tunnels behind the warehouse. The only light was the lamp I carried. I scrambled through the rats and rocks. I smelt something, it was like raw meat. The smell got stronger as I continued into the tunnels. I followed the path round the corner. The smell was overpowering. I climbed down some worn, old steps. I was in a large chamber. I followed the stench to the other side of the room. And in a dark corner, I saw a body, half rotted with a knife in the head. But wait, that was *my* body...

Harry Jachuck (14)
Eastbourne College, Eastbourne

Darkness - Always Waiting

A presence was close. Large portraits stood of boys in waistcoats covered in strands of ivory shadows. Sinister corridors loomed ahead. I sunk into the clean-cut stone and felt a gaze burning through my body. I let my breath go, gasping into the stillness. A high-pitched rasping sound pierced the night. Staring up I could not see. Fear crept along my spine and terror sunk into my heart. The door slammed, spirits of tortured boys groped at the windows of my mind. Where was Tilly? I heard death before I saw it. I could not move - only pray...

Annabel Symes (14)
Eastbourne College, Eastbourne

Untitled

I sped down the dark streets. It was my duty to complete this daunting mission, to prevent grave danger. I had to be quiet, as I crept towards the door to the Prime Minister's office. Gently, I pushed open the door. It was pitch black. As I flicked the light switch, I wished I hadn't.
'Good evening Agent Rogers,' came a hissing voice.
The Prime Minister was gagged and a gun at his temple. In a flash I tackled him off his chair; the gunshot missed him by an inch.
'Nice try,' the hissing louder, a hand on my shoulder.

Imogen Smith (14)
Eastbourne College, Eastbourne

Falling Shards

He sat upon the edge of the building. An almost empty champagne flute at his side.

Flashback
'What are you doing with your life?'
'Enjoying it!'
'Dear God, you're so rash, frittering your fortune away!'
'And it concerns you?'
'I could take away all of this!'

Far off a door slammed. Slowly in his drunken stupor the man stumbled away from the edge. A light tapping became more apparent on the stone. *Smash!* Shards of crystal flew, cutting the man's face. The man stood, and then slipped. The tall, dark figure moved towards him.

Cordelia Stevenson (14)
Eastbourne College, Eastbourne

Escape

He ran; away from the danger, from the pain. He couldn't look back, there wasn't enough time. The wind and rain whipped his face. The footsteps still followed. How? Once he couldn't see it, he'd be free. Holding his top hat, he continued sprinting. The rain began to fade. It was over. He cackled. He cackled continuously until he couldn't breathe. He didn't care. His horrid memories fled with the wind. Expecting a meadow and flowers, he looked back. But it was still there. He had never escaped. Only a madman could believe that they could escape the prison.

Anidampurva Paruchuri (14)
Eastbourne College, Eastbourne

The Last Stop

Nothing but street lamps lit the desolate night as the number thirteen NYC bus, the last bus of the night, approached its stop. Not a soul was stirring under the waiting shelter. The driver started the engine to depart but a brief flicker of light revealed a hooded figure dressed in murky robes and appeared inert. A shiver of fear ran down the driver's spine as he opened the bus doors. The 'thing' lumbered silently and took a seat at the back of the bus. The driver anxiously drove into the barren streets - he was never heard of again.

Will Bearcroft (14)
Eastbourne College, Eastbourne

War Always Wins

His uniform was perfectly ironed, the badges aligned to the exact measures on his broad chest. He stood facing himself in the mirror, staring at his heavily scarred face. He placed his gun down on the cold metallic desk and gazed out the window. There was a creak behind him and the door shook. He cautiously walked over to the door and looked through the hole, nothing. The cold barrel of his gun pushed up against his bare neck. He froze, *click,* as the gun was loaded.
'Hello Colonel,' whispered a familiar voice.

Joe Parish (14)
Eastbourne College, Eastbourne

Untitled

Reverend Bowman surveyed the busy A & E ward with quiet distaste. He slowly backed into an empty store cupboard, unnoticed. The martyr-to-be waited, clutching the wooden cross round his neck. The automatic lights flickered off and he shivered as an icy draught trickled down his spine. Glancing through the crack in the door, he saw nothing and pushed the door open to reveal a completely silent ward. Lights off, all except one, which cast eerie shadows in the gloom. The reverend trembled his way towards the light, and jumped as a trolley squeaked. *Bang!* 'Your plan failed, old man.'

Eleanor Long (14)
Eastbourne College, Eastbourne

The Package

The warehouse loomed out of the settling fog. 'All I have to do is get it.' The heavy metal door creaked as I pushed it ajar. Darkness fell like a blanket as I roamed the dark aisles. This place was like a coffin, cobwebs strung up everywhere. 'Where is it?'
Bang!
'Hello? Is anyone there?'
Now anxious, I carried on searching. Eventually, I found it. Removing it from the shelf I took off the lid. But as I placed it on the hard floor, a chill ran up my spine. I will never forget what happened that night...

Tom Stewart-Blacker (15)
Eastbourne College, Eastbourne

My Little Monster

Sweat slides down my burning forehead. My breath is dragged out of me and the darkness pulls me in. My stumble breaks when my legs freeze, shaking timidly. My home is now my prison. Suddenly, my spine arches. I stand, petrified. Contain it... Pattering footsteps. Contain it... A light breaks on my neck. Contain it... A sinister giggle breaks into my ear. Con... 'Please!' I yell for mercy at my little son, my little monster... An innocent blade twirls on the back of my pale, drained neck. My clear tears tumble into my exhausted blood.

Abby McNally (14)
Eastbourne College, Eastbourne

Joe Dylan

There was a man I knew, Joe Dylan. I always thought he was lying about it. Maybe it was the way he'd said it. He was medium height, dark grey hair, no glasses or walking stick and paper-white skin, almost like a ghost. The house he lived in was old, but not as old as him. I could never guess his age. I used to hear howling at night when I was younger, I always thought it was my dog. I'm only recently discovering it was him. People only now tell me why they're so glad he's long gone.

Connie Crossland (15)
Eastbourne College, Eastbourne

Woods

The policeman walked cautiously through the woods. His trembling hand grabbed continuously at his belt which contained his gun. His head felt heavy and his chest ached from the accelerated pounding of his heart. It wasn't long ago that he had heard the screams. They were desperate screams, those that belong to somebody who is being tortured to death. As he continued walking he could hear somebody or something whispering. He couldn't tell what.

Alice Nicole Venturelli (15)
Eastbourne College, Eastbourne

THE CITY THAT NEVER SLEEPS

He slouched in his wooden pew. The city never slept, and neither did he. His eyes were shut but he saw everything. The long silver blade by his bare foot, still unclean from its last job. The reflected city lights danced off its mirror. The suicidal rope that had wrapped around many necks and presented the gift of death lay dormant beneath the blanket of dust that slept upon it. His eyes fluttered open, bloodshot and crazed as he reached with trembling brittle fingers for his favourite one of all.

JESSECCA CHAPMAN (14)
Eastbourne College, Eastbourne

THE EXPERIMENT

Her body shook violently as she slept. He knew what was in her head as he watched her quivering face contorted in pain. Her silent screams sliced through him as he stood, feeding more liquid into her bloody, foaming mouth. She was, after all, only his science experiment. The sly grin faded from his face as her convulsions stopped and her breathing rate lowered. He had killed her, although that wasn't what worried him. His experiment had failed... again. He had really thought he had got it right this time. Rage washed over him and he kicked her limp body.

ISABELLE NEWTON (14)
Eastbourne College, Eastbourne

Waiting Room

Uncomfortably I sat on the tough leather waiting chairs. The automatic door creaked open. A man in torn clothes limped in. The room dimmed down. His smell filled the room like a disease. He walked forward lamely, dragging one of his feet behind him towards the end of the corridor. He jostled through the door till he was not visible, but leaving a trail of his vile smell behind. Slowly faint screams grew louder, blurting through the whole hospital. What was wrong with the incomprehensible man?

Alfie Pagram (14)
Eastbourne College, Eastbourne

Snap

Snap! The gleaming bright sun peeking through and the neon background were combined. In the top left-hand corner I could make out a shadow. I looked up - nothing. Maybe it was the faulty camera. *Snap!* The next wall. Red, blues and greens splattered. Again the black shadow, this time it was closer. I looked up - nothing. I was surrounded by four walls with a narrow alley. *Snap! Snap! Snap!* It wasn't a faulty camera...

Sophie Stephenson (15)
Eastbourne College, Eastbourne

Tinted Windows

My ears were being sliced off by the silent wind. The birds weren't so lively today. In fact, nothing about this place was lively. I pursed my lips and whistled softly. The sound I made was murdered by the wind. I tucked my hands into my pocket and kicked around at the rubble on the old dusty road. A car engine crept up over my left shoulder. With tinted front windows, I only saw a pale face with wide brown eyes staring desperately back at me from the back seat. It kept glaring at me. Why?

Freya Cournane (15)
Eastbourne College, Eastbourne

Four Knocks

I heard about an IT technician in this company that knocks a rhythm of four whenever he does anything. Today, after finishing my project, I realised that everyone had left. I crawled to the lift exhausted. Behind me I heard four knocks. Walking out the building, I could still hear the strange rhythm. As I went, the four beats followed me becoming clearer and louder. Finally in an alley that leads me to my home, the knocks stopped. I felt so relieved that I took a deep breath. After the break, came another four knocks. But I can't hear it anymore.

Bill Cao (15)
Eastbourne College, Eastbourne

The Night It All Happened

I had my camera at the ready, my eyes glaring into all corners of the dark, dingy, dangerous room. My heartbeat was as loud as a drum. Spiders and other insects were creeping through the doorway. My hands were shaking rapidly. *Crash!* A bolt of lightning lit the room up and, with a three second interval, the thunder smashed the stained-glass window of the cold warehouse. As I jolted, I fell onto something, it was slimy and felt wet. My camera suddenly flashed. All of a sudden a picture appeared on the camera screen, and it was her.

Ella Hemming (13)
Eastbourne College, Eastbourne

City By Night

Only the skyscraper's light filled the derelict city. The moonlight was dead. My hands clasped the banister of the city steps. Black shadows clung to my footsteps like weights dragging on the ground. I heard a deep, quiet voice. It was behind me. I looked back only to see a sea of mist. A yellow cab slowly pulled up behind me. My face went pale as a hand slammed against the window. The breath mark stained the window and engraved in it, read something terrible. The skyscraper's light flickered off; the only light was coming from the yellow cab.

Maisie Williams (14)
Eastbourne College, Eastbourne

The Night Bus Terror

It was pitch black outside, you couldn't see anything but flickering lights from the bus. Nobody knew the driver. What was he called? Where was he from? There was always something covering his face along with a cloak. There were never any passengers until one night, a nurse decided to take a journey. She could see his eyes, but not his face. She sat in the back with springs hanging out of the seats and that's when she saw the eyes outside the bus and the driver was gone. The bus would crash into the hospital she'd just come from.

Alfredo Vazquez (14)
Eastbourne College, Eastbourne

Abandoned Warehouse

He was taking pictures in an abandoned warehouse. The strange thing about this warehouse was that every picture he took had something on it that you wouldn't see with your own eyes. There was a sort of creature that appeared on camera. He checked the lens to make sure there wasn't any dirt on it, but there wasn't. Each picture the shadow would get closer. On his last picture the shadow was right in front of him. He suddenly felt something cold on his back... like a hand... But he was alone - maybe he wasn't.

Arno Peller (14)
Eastbourne College, Eastbourne

Demon

He's always there, in the corner of my eye, planted on the bench. The man barely speaks. His eyes are dark like midnight and his grin scares us all. Why does he call her name? 'Emily?' he calls out. Nobody knows where he goes to, he just disappears like dust. He's put a trance on us all. He has wiped our minds blank. All I can recall is that night in the park when he entered at six and left at ten. Soon after his presence was gone. The clock ticked midnight, and the man came back.

Maddie Perrett (13)
Eastbourne College, Eastbourne

The Swing

We went to the playground every Wednesday after school. It was 4:30pm. I put little Jonny on the swing. I pushed him a couple of times then realised there was no one in the playground. I left Jonny on the swing to help Big Ben onto the climbing wall. When I got back to Jonny he had changed. He had a cut on his lip and on his chin. He had a scary look on his face like the ones you see in horror movies. I asked what was wrong but he did not speak. He never spoke again after that.

Oliver Harvey (13)
Eastbourne College, Eastbourne

A Woman In The Street

It was late. A woman was walking home with her friends. They were laughing. When her friends were near their houses, they left and the woman carried on, alone. She was laughing for a bit. Suddenly she felt like somebody was staring at her. She looked back. Nobody was there. She looked back again. She saw a street light flashing... and a man wearing a black hood... The woman stopped. She turned around. 'Who's there?' she shouted. But nobody was around. The street light didn't work. When she turned back, she saw a man right in front of her...

Timur Mikhaylov (13)
Eastbourne College, Eastbourne

Whose Daughter?

It was a dark and calm night. The poor man was picking up some milk from the store. On the way back he heard a little girl singing. Her voice was weak. He looked around but nobody was there. The voice almost hypnotised the man, like a serenade. The voice led him to an abandoned home. At the end of the corridor there was a room. In the room a shadow of a girl was playing with a doll. The door slammed shut. The only trace of the man was the smashed milk bottle at the doorstep of the house.

Ashraf Owasil (13)
Eastbourne College, Eastbourne

The Cabin

There was a cabin that was dark and gloomy. I went to the door. I knocked, the door opened. I looked inside, there wasn't anybody there. I stepped inside, the door slammed behind me. A shiver went down my spine. I tried to open the door but I couldn't. Suddenly I heard a blood-curdling scream, it sounded like my mum. I followed the sound and found her. I walked very slowly towards her. She looked at me, her eyes were as white as snow and she screamed, 'There is no escape.'
I said, 'There is no escape from what?'

Reece Ord (13)
Hospital Education Service, Coventry

The Hand

It was twelve o'clock at night. The full moon crept out from the misty fog. I walked home through the woods. The more I walked the more trees that fell closely to me. I lost my path so I kept walking forwards. It started to rain with the thunder and lightning launching at me. Then I ran, trying to find shelter. Then I paused. I shivered. I came up to a rusty gate. I heard the howl of the wolves. I felt the cold shivering on me. A wet, cold hand touched my shoulder. Then it crawled to my neck...

Shriya Rajpara (11)
Hospital Education Service, Coventry

Can War Really Be Justified?

I cradled the child in my arms as the guns were still going off. Her family was nowhere to be seen. I felt how frozen her frail body was. This really made me think, *can war really be justified?* At this point I knew it was my duty to take care of her, just like my own child. She had nothing left, not even her mother or father. I could see the devastation in her eyes as she looked deeply into my eyes. She had blood pouring out of her stomach and she knew she needed help quick!

Ellie-Mae Turner (15)
Hospital Education Service, Coventry

Revenge!

It was a dark, gloomy Tuesday morning and there was a linger of green fog polluting the streets of London. Casper was patrolling around Westminster in search of his next victim. He would always try to steal cash or a luxury item. He was facing Big Ben as the bells rang to signal it was ten o'clock. Casper was glaring across the street, looking for vulnerable people, but then he felt a sharp pain digging into his back. He turned around and noticed that the pain had vanished. Also there was no damage or any sign of an obvious culprit.

Harry Horbury (14)
Hospital Education Service, Coventry

The Knocker

My heart hammered against my chest as my breathing became shallow. Eyes wide, I tried to take in all the possible outcomes. A dark figure on the black screen of my television caught my eye. Once again I turned around to see what was behind me, nothing was there. A knocking sound disturbed my thoughts; silence engulfed me as I waited for another knock. Nothing happened. My heart stopped cold and I involuntarily held my breath. Standing very still I looked towards my door. The figure I'd been seeing all night was standing right there, staring at me.

Bethany Leigh Wilson (14)
Hospital Education Service, Coventry

Barwell Massacre

In the small town of Barwell everyone was full of joy. Suddenly darkness rose. No one was about, only me. All you could hear was the light flickering like a candle. The atmosphere was gloomy. Fog started to creep in. All I could see was a crowd of people. I stood petrified. They angrily charged towards me. What was I supposed to do? I could feel tension getting stronger. I could see shadows of big swords and axes. I needed to do something. I could see the big crowd charging forward. The sweat dripped from my face. What happened next?

Holly Neale (14)
Hospital Education Service, Coventry

Little Boy Lost

A carpet of leaves, scattered on the forest floor, crunched and rustled as she frantically ran through the moonlit shadows. She stopped for a minute and gasped to catch her breath, which could clearly be seen in the cold night air. She needed to think about what she had just witnessed: a small, frail little boy, no older than five, with ice-white skin and dark sunken eyes stood amongst the trees in the distance staring at her. She turned. She ran. Seconds later he stood in her path. A little boy lost, or a ghost?

Demi Swindin (15)
Hospital Education Service, Coventry

The Shadow Beast

There I was staring at the dark, shadowy figure. All I could see of the beast was its red glowing eyes. It lurked in the corner of the room making a deafening, screeching, high-pitched sound. I backed away, frightened, but it pulled on my hand. I thought of trying to escape but I was afraid of what was outside, because I could hear terrifying sounds whizzing, whooshing and rumbling.
Suddenly a figure emerged from outside the room. It began to speak.
'Josh, your antibiotics are finished.'
I remembered I was in hospital and the shadow beast was my drip!

Joshua Womble
Hospital Education Service, Coventry

Trick Or Treat

John and Tom were trick or treating. Little did they know it was their last laugh. They approached a mysterious mansion. As John cautiously knocked on the door, the ground swallowed him. Tom was deafened by the scream of his soul. The door opened with a screech. Tom was grabbed viciously by a monstrous hand. Tom clawed at it, wailing as he was dragged in. In the corner of his eye, Tom could see a slumped, pale body. Trembling, Tom cautiously crept towards it, his eyes hardly open. As it suddenly clenched Tom's shuddering leg, his soul exited his body...

Layton Simmons (12)
Hospital Education Service, Coventry

The Eyes

My arms began trembling as I crept nervously down the stairs. A sharp tingly feeling flowed through my body. My ears twitched as they picked up a peculiar muffled whispering sound. I reached the bottom of the stairs. It was cast with darkness. I felt on edge. I could sense that someone had their eyes on me. I looked around the room. A broad shadowed figure with vicious, red eyes was standing there in the corner, glaring at me. I froze. It began to get closer, its eyes growing wider. My body grew weaker - I couldn't move...

Chloe Rumming (14)
Hospital Education Service, Coventry

Bang...

My face was up against the rough concrete. A drop of blood fell in front of my eyes. It was too dark to see anything except for the lights on the Eiffel Tower. He stood against my body and reloaded his gun. He stared at my body, checking if I was dead. Butterflies were having a disco in my stomach. The world was spinning. The man bent down and grabbed my wrist to check my pulse. He stood back up. *Bang!* Everything went dark.

Izzy Alexander (11)
Hospital Education Service, Coventry

Forbidden Graveyard

As I was about to turn the corner something caught my eye... the moonlit graveyard, ancient and abandoned. Ominous grey clouds filled the charcoal sky, while the glowing cemetery shone in the distance, luring me towards it. Nervously I swung open the ivy-covered gate which creaked on its rusted hinges. Wisps of crisp cold air sent shivers down my spine as it murmured in my ears, as if it was warning me to turn back. I pushed on forwards weaving my way cautiously through the eroded gravestones, decrepit and layered with blanket upon blanket of furry green moss.

Serena Dha (14)
Hospital Education Service, Coventry

Jungle Terror

I awake to a bird-eating tarantula scurrying across my cold, damp face. I sit hopelessly waiting for the spider to crawl off. Suddenly, in the distance, I spot a dark figure running towards me. I jump to my feet, trembling in fear. I start to run but when I turn there's nothing there. I slouch down behind a tree in relief. Suddenly, I feel something slithering up my spine. I turn and see a tiger snake staring at me. Then, out of nowhere, a blade just skims my face. It's a native American. I run in fear with him following.

Edward Townsend Johnson (13)
Hospital Education Service, Coventry

Zombie

On my way home from school I was walking with my brother, Tank, in the frosty, gloomy fog. We couldn't see then the fog cleared. On this very day, Friday 13th, 4 o'clock, my mum would be home. We were at St Mary's Church in the graveyard. Then we heard screaming, shouting, hissing, Shouting of our names. I was scared! They were zombies. As we got to the car Tank got bitten but nobody knew. When we got home Mum was happy to see us, well, for now. As Tank had been bitten, it would affect the entire human race.

Jacob James Cooke (12)
Hospital Education Service, Coventry

HELP!

Wind blows through my hair as I stumble towards the door, knees covered in scars and cuts dripping with blood. As I reach for the brass lion door knocker, I notice two gleaming red eyes, staring down from the window above. I see shadows moving in the bushes. *It's just your eyes,* I think, *you're tired.* A gust of wind flings open the door, creaking loudly as it goes. A shiver travels down my spine. A loud whisper runs through my head. 'We've been expecting you.' Two pale, bloody hands touch my shoulders. Icy breath down my neck. I fall.

CAITLIN BATCHELOR (11)
Hospital Education Service, Coventry

SCREAM HOUSE

I walked down the street and I heard a scream. Who was it and why was it coming from my granny's house? I was thinking over and over about what had happened, I knew it: I was going to sneak off to my granny's house with my spy kit. I would solve this mystery once and for all. I stood on the mat, my finger on the doorbell. I pushed my finger but no sound came. I leaned over to get the spare key that was under the mat, then the door opened. A man in a cape stood there...

ANNA SILVER
Kent College, Canterbury

I Can See Right Through You

I woke up shivering. My nails had turned icy blue and my lips were dripping with blood. Creeping quietly to wash my face, I stopped in my tracks and snuck a glance at the full sized mirror; it was translucent and therefore I saw an eerie figure in an oversized nightie. Black liquid snaked down pale skin and dark hair stuck to a sweaty face. Slowly, it lifted its hand and said, 'It's the end...' Suddenly the mirror cracked and the thing collapsed... It was only me after a night out.

Reese Robinson (12)
Kent College, Canterbury

The Knife

A slender man is following me. It is 19.30 on the 21st June. I'm on the tube with the slender man. He is following me. It is now dark, I'm at my last stop on the tube. The slender man is still here. He has a knife dripping with blood. I am walking to the bus stop. I have now got onto the bus, five minutes until I am home. It's been four minutes and I'm getting off the bus. I've got home and my mum, dad and brother are dead. Slender and I love to kill.

Harry Devereux (11)
Kent College, Canterbury

Second

Wind was whistling tonight, unlike any other night. Animals moaning. I knew something didn't feel right. My hands frozen. A silhouette appeared in the corner of my eye. I tried to turn but my body wouldn't move, my fear terrified me. The silhouette had gone. I turned around, a scarred figure stood at my feet.
'I was first, you are second.' The man fell to the floor, blood surrounding my feet. I fell fearfully. A figure stood over me, his right hand covered in blood and his left was holding a gun. He was first, you are second.

Christopher Figgis (11)
Kent College, Canterbury

Blood Tears

I walked past the playground. Toddlers fled. I walked towards the graveyard. Home. I went to my room, to the mirror. I looked at the picture of me with Mother. That was before it happened. Now I feel empty without fear. Not mine, someone else's. I look in the mirror. I see blood, dripping down my face. My past is the past. I have become myself now. The sun set. I went outside. There was someone outside. *Perfect,* I thought. I walked up to him, put my cobwebbed hand on his shoulder. He screamed. 'Hello, ready to die?' I said.

Daisy O'Connor
Kent College, Canterbury

Fish And Chips?

I glanced around at the bleak fairground. It had long since been deserted. Where are the gates? Where are the people? I could die for food right now. The roller coasters were off, the lights were on standby. I went to where I knew the gates would be. I reached for the rusty metal latch. I twisted the handle. *Click!* Oh no, locked! I suddenly heard a voice. 'Fish and chips, fish and chips!' I'm not alone. I don't know what's worse. I turned around and saw a man dripping with blood. He held a skewer to my neck...

Eleanor Lucy Buchanan (11)
Kent College, Canterbury

Cold Hands And Snowy White Eyes

I heard footsteps. Cold hands stroked my shoulder. The woods began enclosing around me. I ran. Branches snapped beneath my feet, sending shivers up my spine. Snowy white eyes appeared in amongst the gloomy fog of the forest. I stopped dead in my tracks. The sound of my heavy breathing seemed to be the only sound for miles. Then the eyes disappeared. The cold hands were back. Slowly they moved, holding my neck. The grip got tighter. My scream was silent. I gasped for breath but it was no use. 'I told you I would come for you...'

Gabrielle Cornelius-Merrell (11)
Kent College, Canterbury

Trapped In My Own Body

As a kid I always wanted to go to Egypt. Now I'm not so sure... Sand keeps blowing in my eyes and anyway, I'm only here because of my dad's job (he is an explorer). We're at Tutankhamun's tomb... but where is Dad? Suddenly he's gone and I hear laughter bouncing around the stony walls. I feel a chill run for its life down my spine and I fear I should run too. A wrinkled hand reaches out and I can't feel my heartbeat anymore. I fall to the ground, expecting death, but I'm still alive, on the inside.

Amy Gallagher (11)
Kent College, Canterbury

Possessed

I reached for the dagger. She let out a strangled moan, backing away from me, begging, pleading. It wasn't real, it was only a pretence, one that the devil hoped I would fall for and foolishly spare her so that he would have the opportunity to take me for his own. I advanced towards her, showing no mercy as I flung her to the floor. An animal scream escaped her lips. With one last pitiful whimper I struck the dagger into her chest, piercing through the skin and twisting it, taking away the last life of the devil within.

Antoinette Chastang
Kent College, Canterbury

Peek-A-Boo!

The thunder struck twelve. I started to walk away from the party! My friends had left me in the tingling rain. Ten minutes to my nice warm bed. I took one step. As I did so, a cold wet hand took my shoulder. I turned around, it was only my friend Lisa. But Lisa wasn't the same. She was holding a cracked doll without eyes. Then I realised Lisa had taken the doll's eyes and put them where her eyes should have been. I screamed and ran home where a doll was waiting for me. A doll without eyes...

Olivia Aylwin (12)
Kent College, Canterbury

Dear Diary Of Hell

Today the worst thing happened, a boy walked up to me and... he spoke in a quiet voice, 'I know your secret.'
My legs gave way. I dropped to the floor, screaming for help. I couldn't stop. I felt my life was in danger. As the nurse came to take me away he raised an eyebrow and *bang!* He was gone. I started panting and my throat was swelling, I felt death roll down my throat and it was reaching my heart. Then I realised it was you. You did this to me...

Freya Buckley (11)
Kent College, Canterbury

ABANDONED

I have been dropped off in the middle of nowhere. My family has had enough of me. I know I am going to die out here. The sun is incredibly bright but it's not hot. There is a very cold ice illusion on the floor but it's not cold. I may as well just kill myself in a quicker way than starving. This climate is so weird and strange, what shall I do out here? I start to run for completely no reason. I run, run, run. The world under me disappears then I fall, fall, fall.

SAM SMITH (12)
Kent College, Canterbury

BANG

Bang!
'Wait!' he said.
'I hear footsteps,' I said to myself quietly.
'Don't move,' whispered a voice from behind me.
I wasn't alone. In a wood, not alone, what else could be worse?
'Why?' I replied in a husky, whispering voice.
'Just don't move.'
Suddenly, as this was said, the whole wood echoed with the thought of someone. I was scared. I am never scared. But I was scared.
'What do I do? What do I do?' I tried to say quietly but it came out loud. Before they said something back I felt a wrinkled hand on my shoulder...

JESS MCMEEKING (11)
Kent College, Canterbury

Dad, Don't Kill Me

He could hear the girl breathe slowly. Carefully he crept in, without making a sound. He neared the bed, getting closer by the second. When he was a few centimetres away from the girl's bed, he pulled down his hood revealing his torn face and out of his pocket came a dagger covered in blood from his previous victim. Just as he was about to do the deed, the girl rolled over and in her sleep said, 'Dad, I know it's you. Don't kill me, it's happening anyway,' and with that the girl rolled over and died in his arms.

Ella Jain (12)
Kent College, Canterbury

Graveyard Of Hell

Walking through the graveyard, I heard the screams of all the bodies yelling for help as the masked devil took the souls of the innocent humans. I stepped slowly, walking towards a black, metal gate. Suddenly something squished under my feet. I shone my torch down to see what I had squished. A head, an actual head! I ran towards the gate, seeing the light of the street. The gate was getting closer. It was open. However, suddenly, *bang!* Someone or something had closed the gate. I heard a cackle and chains rumbling. Then I realised, I would not get out.

Sasha Godden (12)
Kent College, Canterbury

He Disappeared

I stared at the outline of myself in the mirror which gradually began to move with the silhouette of a man outside. He walked along the street just like a ghost. I blinked. I blinked again but this time the contours of a human stood in front of me. A silent scream creaked out through the seam of my lips. The wind began to howl and fog was creeping in. It was like a signal of death. 'Is it you, Dad?'
'No sweetheart, it's me, the ghost of your death!' He disappeared and so did I.

Emily Hanson (11)
Kent College, Canterbury

Don't Worry, It Will Be Over Soon...

Bam! Life hit me right where it hurt - my heart. It fell out of place and *splat!* It was on the floor. Alone. Home alone. But was I? I strolled into the living room to find a limp silhouette. 'Daddy?' No reply. I turned on the light. Dead! I ran up to my room. 'Mummy?' No reply. Was she sleeping? No... I felt no pulse. My heart stopped, similar to hers. My room was the only place where I felt safe. I sat at the bottom of the stairs, turned around. There they stood... 'But you're dead...'
That was my end...

Channice Marks (12)
Kent College, Canterbury

The Sniper

The wind hissed in his ears as each step he took seemed to take him closer to death. His pursuers were showing no sign of tiredness, determination gleaming in their eyes. One of them, tall, dressed in dark camouflage fatigues, raised his machine gun and opened fire. The bullets whizzed past him, rattling against a metallic plate and bouncing off. Then, out of the corner of his eye, he saw a sniper taking aim. His finger squeezed the trigger, the shot rang, the bullet whizzing towards him. It seemed already covered with his blood. There was no possible escape, unless...

Mickaël Jacques Topiol (13)
Kew House School, Brentford

Legend Of The Seven Stones

Ben was alone. The thick moss from the tree he was leaning on felt moist against his torn, filthy T-shirt. At last Ben was ready to start again, but strangely he felt like he was being watched. And then he felt it: breathing. It sounded like it was coming from far away and it was gradually getting closer and louder. The hackles on the back of Ben's neck were rising as he felt the breathing getting closer until, at last, he felt it on the nape of his neck. Ben looked to his left, and there stood his enemy, glaring.

Emerson Loat (14)
Kew House School, Brentford

The Follower

Cautiously I walked along a dismally lit path towards a castle. *Crunch!* The maroon leaves and sticks shattered into fragments as I stepped on them. The sounds repeated themselves from behind me. I could hear heavy breathing. Sprinting for my life, I heard a huge groan and felt like I was being spied on and followed by the undead or even a serial killer. Arriving quickly at the castle, I went inside, slammed the door behind me, locked it and backed away. As I backed away, a hand rested upon my shoulder and as I turned, I screamed, 'Help me!'

Rajan Matharu (15)
Kew House School, Brentford

The Untold Scene

The shrieking noise crept upon her without a warning. Alone in the darkness she sat, waiting for the company to arrive. *Bang!* That was the sound of her back door. She recognised it vividly. She rushed to her telephone and held it firmly. She slid through her kitchen towards the mysterious darkness. To her surprise, she saw nothing but the outdoor street lamp shining through the window. Slowly she felt a cold barrel of a pistol crawl up on her temple.

Josephine Aurik (13)
Kew House School, Brentford

Silhouette

Walls of white surrounded me. I felt fear rising in my throat but quickly swallowed it down. With a swift survey I soon realised there was something fundamentally wrong with the room: it had no door - no way in and no way out. So how did I get here? An ominous grey shadow crept up the blank walls, gradually consuming the entire wall and replacing sterile white with stormy grey. My eyes locked on the wall, unable to bring myself to look at the source of the silhouette; after all I was alone, wasn't I? I spun around. I wasn't...

Holly Harvey (13)
Kew House School, Brentford

Running, But Never Escaping

I run; my footsteps echo in my ears and shatter the eerie silence around me, like the first bolt of lightning in a vicious storm. *Thud! Thud!* I run faster still, past lifeless ivy, past decaying branches and past the derelict mansion, almost invisible under the weeds. I put on an extra burst of speed as I pass its graveyard-like grounds. Nevertheless, a feeling of icy cold, like a ghost, passes through me. Suddenly an ivy branch curls around my leg and I fall, dingy mud filling my lungs, suffocating me. Claws tear at my shoulder; white-hot pain sears everywhere...

Sarah Makhmudova (12)
Kew House School, Brentford

Alone

I walked across the deserted bridge, a cold hard wind echoed in my ears. The only light was the weak light that the full moon emitted. Shivers ran down my spine for I felt a sudden consciousness of being followed. I looked to my side, a second shadow suddenly flickered. I looked around myself. With a quick movement of my head, I confirmed I was alone, completely alone. Or was I? Yes of course I was, how could I not be? I kept telling myself this but suddenly I felt a hand on my shoulder, claws dug into my flesh.

Emilie Grol (14)
Kew House School, Brentford

Who Are You?

I ran as fast as a hare. The figure was catching up and I was tiring. What was it? As I turned the corner I came colliding into a hard object, which seemed to be alive. It couldn't have been a tree, because it was too small, and it couldn't have been any kind of animal, because it was too big. I backed away, nervous. What seemed to be an arm reached out and grabbed my shoulder. 'Come with me child,' it whispered.
'Who are you?' I asked.
'Does it matter? No one will ever know you have gone...'

Felix Scott (13)
Kew House School, Brentford

Painful Song

Scraping its heels along the floorboards, the ebony silhouette gets closer towards my rustic shield of a bedroom door. A frantic spider deviously crawls up my back, pricking each vertebrae in my spine with ultimate fear. Closer! Devilish shadows perform a gruesome tale straining my glacial eyes. *Thud!* Nerves churn up my throat, innards throbbing when the sickening halt sounds through the door. The painful song of its feet has stopped but it doesn't bring relief, just lonely shrieks. Venomous snakes slither through crimson blood, poisoning every bone to become weak and afraid. The doorknob turns. Gone.

Willow Murray (12)
Kew House School, Brentford

Into The Woods

The sky is darkening and the sun is fading. I don't know what to do. Alice told me she would be there by five and all I could see were miles and miles of trees. I felt that someone was watching me so swiftly I turned to spectate around me. *Snap!* The sound of a twig snapping in half rang in my ears. 'Alice? I'm over here!' It was probably a bad idea to say that and one more time I heard another twig snap but this time it was right behind me. I knew this was my last... breath.

Leena Tarabulsi (12)
Kew House School, Brentford

The Dark Knight

It was a dark night, the sky was a black hole in space. Quickly we got into the building. I saw someone or something run after us. It was tall, black and with blood all over it. *Bang!* was the sound when this creature knocked on the door and started to look around. He smelt like rubbish, it was disgusting. He almost found us. We were in shock when we saw its face but before he killed us and tried to do something - from nowhere - *Bang!* Daddy!

Harel Natan (12)
Kew House School, Brentford

Curse Of The Dangerous Wolf

Whilst investigating the death of a local policeman, a pretty girl called Lydia Martin and her boyfriend Stiles Stilinski uncover a legend about a dangerous wolf throughout California, America.
Two days later, Stiles and Lydia spot a dark shadow. Suddenly, Lydia feels a huge, bloody bite on her leg and gets a flashback into her mind. At one of the game stores, an animal of some sort with red eyes ran past her car. What if this was the creature? Slowly her hazel-green, big eyes closed and Stile knew they were closing forever. Tears rolled down.

Hanne Ellemann (12)
Kew House School, Brentford

The Shadow

Waking up, I think I feel a gentle but sudden scratch against my bed. I get out of my bed and I see a shadow drifting down the hall. The soft call of the shadow makes me blunder towards it. I resist a bit longer but after a minute or two it goes down the stairs. I follow. It takes me through the kitchen and into the living room. Gently it opens the door and leads me into the big, dark, frightening and dangerous world. Down the patio and up the road and into the abyss of its dark lair.

Georgie Clarke (12)
Kew House School, Brentford

The Nightmare Of A Joke

We finally arrived at camp for D of E. Along the way we kept joking about the black cat that apparently a local farmer saw. We jumped into our tent with full bellies after having kebabs and toasted marshmallows. Later on that night I heard some rummaging from outside. 'What's that noise?' I quickly opened the flap up. It was only then I saw a black shadow appear. *No, it couldn't be.* A shiver went down my spine. We peeped out again, but this time a strange creature came closer and closer to our tent - the joke was real...

William Patrick Arthur Clarke
Kew House School, Brentford

It Was Meant To Be A Prank

I was going to prank Joe. I bent down to do my shoelace. 'One sec, I'm just doing my laces. You go on.'
Joe walked.
Yes! I thought. I ran home and knocked on the door.
My mum opened the door. 'Hi, ummm... where's Joe?' Mum asked.
'I'm playing a prank on him, Mum,' I said giggling.
'Go and get Joe now!' Mum shouted.
I ran back the way we came. When I got there I saw Joe sitting in front. He stood up and looked into my eyes. His were black. He gripped my shirt. 'This is no prank!' *Thud!*

Freddie Fraser-Grante (12)
Kew House School, Brentford

The Creak

Creak! I sat up in bed. The haunted house made me feel unsettled as I walked down the stairs in the block. Whenever I was about to step there was a creak. I'd step, no noise. I'd be about to step - *creak!*
I panicked, wondering what on earth was making the sound. I ran back into bed and pulled the covers over my head. My door creaked. Silence for five minutes. I lay absolutely still. Not making the smallest twitch or movement of any kind. I pulled off the cover and looked up. He'd found me. He'd creak no more.

Zachary Jackson
Kew House School, Brentford

The Voice

Running for hours, sweat trickling down my forehead. I'm not sure what I'm running from. It's the voice in my head. I cannot think, its threatening voice is always in my ear. It whispers, 'You cannot hide, I'm coming for you,' followed by an evil chuckle. I'm lost, desperate for help, but the towns I'm running through are like endless graveyards. Suddenly, a petrifying ghost-like creature grabs my collar and holds a knife by my throat, its cold breath condensing on my blood-drained skin, sending shivers down my spine. I know this is the end.. The voice finishes me.

Joseph Henry Hall (12)
Kew House School, Brentford

The Haunted House

I shiver as the wind blows against my bare arms. The house before me screeches with every blow, as if it might fall any minute. I have to do this. I take a deep breath and with the slightest bit of hesitation I slowly twist the doorknob counter-clockwise, expecting it to creak so loudly it will wake the dead. But it opens easily, without a sound. Just as I step into the house, the doors shut behind me with a deafening bang and before I have time to look behind me, an icy, clawed hand digs into my shoulder.

Daniela Buriak (13)
Kew House School, Brentford

The Lurking Shadow

What was that? Was it an apparition? I tucked myself back into bed and pretended to be asleep. An arm? It disappeared. The door handle started to twist. Gently it opened. A tall slender figure appeared and glared at me as I quivered. Silently, the figure approached. Still I couldn't see what it was or what it looked like. The figure then drooped over my face. 'I know you're awake!' A hand dragged across my covers...

Ben Banks (12)
Kew House School, Brentford

The Silent Blood Wood

She stepped on the crisp, white ground. Her thin finger pulsed crimson blood, dripping onto the snow-covered earth. The wind howled, the bright blue eyes watching her every step from behind. She still walked, entering the heart of the woods, the round, shining moon glowing down from the black midnight sky. An animal howled. The padding of grey, rough paws scuffed the silent snow. The blue eyes fixated on her. The blood still dripping, calling to the creature, taunting him. The creature lost all control... The blood spattered everywhere on the snow in the once more silent Blood Wood.

Phoebe Botwood (12)
Kew House School, Brentford

The Day I Died

November 25th. The day I died! It was an ordinary day, but like no other. I was outside my usual bus stop when it happened. I noticed a man in a black hat, black leather gloves and a black overcoat. He stood under a flickering lamppost. I peered in; all I could see was a grin. I looked away then looked back. He was gone! Suddenly, I felt something sharp go into my back. I felt liquid trickle down my spine. I heard a devilish laugh, and he said, 'Your family's next.'

Olly Porteous (12)
Kew House School, Brentford

Our New House

Our new house! It looked as if it could do with some re-doing on the outside but I thought it might look more appealing on the inside. I was wrong. Inside felt and appeared to be as haunting and spine-tingling as from the outside. It all just got worse from then. Things were breaking mysteriously, there were voices. It was how you would imagine a haunted house to be like. One night, it all got too much. I heard loud whispers. Spirits. Just then, there was a face. Breathing into my soul was a dead and disfigured face.

Amiya Sitlani (13)
Kew House School, Brentford

Signs...

Alex was lying in bed, listening to his clock. Every tick seemed to get slower until it eventually stopped. He sat up, confused, trying to find the light switch. He touched something cold and wooden. He turned on the light and he looked at the clock. It wasn't broken, it was new. Then looking to the wall, he saw a sign saying, 'Hello Alex, you don't know me but I know you. I'm here for you. Close your eyes, Alex. Close your eyes. Oh yeah and don't look up.'

Ruby Radigund Eliot (12)
Kew House School, Brentford

The Endless Shadows

Sweat trickled down the nape of my neck. Biting my tongue, I spat as I tasted crimson blood. Pouring out of my mouth, the blood continued like an endless waterfall. I furiously wiped my face, smearing the liquid like war paint. Darkness painted my surroundings and that's when I felt the gaze of a thousand eyes. Staring up into a charcoal darkness, I glimpsed a pair of feral eyes. They fixed on mine and my heart pounded like a drum. Then, in a swift movement, the eyes pounced. The darkness enticed me and so I succumbed to the endless shadows.

Cleo Packham (12)
Kew House School, Brentford

The Misty Woods

Walking through the misty woods I could hear shrieks coming from all different directions. Some of the shrieks had my name in them. I was chilled to the core. I just had to keep reciting in my head, 'I'm fine, it's just the wind. I'm fine, it's just the wind.' Soon, after a short period of time the reciting method failed. I was panicking so much I could hear my heartbeat getting louder and louder. Running frantically through the forest I thought to myself silently, *will I ever see the light of day again?*

Daphne Michaelides (13)
Kew House School, Brentford

The Wolf Run

The fog crept out from behind the trees, I ran and ran, but the panting of the wolves grew: closer, closer, closer. I charged through the woods with no luck. I made the mistake of looking back. They were fifty metres away now, picking up pace. I turned around and just managed to dodge a tree. *How long have I been running,* I thought, *an hour, two hours?* Long enough to feel like I couldn't go any further. I felt like my life would last for as long as I could run. I charged through the woods, until, I fell.

Christopher Behnert-Lackner (12)
Kew House School, Brentford

The Shop

I was running from the shop knowing that someone was killed there after I heard that loud screech from an old woman. I ran through the gardens hoping to get to my apartment as soon as possible. 'I'm going to get you!' I heard loudly from the distance. I sprinted as fast as my legs could carry me. I tripped over a plant pot in the garden. I fell and noticed my knee was badly grazed but I kept running. Eventually I got to my apartment complex. I sprinted up the stairs to my door. I opened it. 'You want a biscuit, child?'

Marco Landazabal (13)
Kew House School, Brentford

Slapped In The Stalls

I ran into the bathroom; things were going worse than I thought. I locked the stall door and sat in silence for what seemed like hours. I came out, slowly, unlocking the stall door and opening it. Suddenly I was slapped, but no one was there. I looked in the mirror. There was a person standing behind me. They looked... faded. A ghost! 'Hello,' I called out, still staring in the mirror. Falling over, my life flashed before my eyes. Was this the end? I was bleeding. Blood filled the room. I was going to die but then something changed...

Florence Hughes (12)
Kew House School, Brentford

The Footsteps

Night is starting to creep in and I feel the cool wind whip across my face. I search for shelter. I see an old church through the gloom. I walk to the bulky door and give it a push. It opens... slowly. I wedge a rock under the door to keep it open and for light. I walk inside. The air is stale and rotten. The stained glass windows cast evil shadows... like a skull in a dress. Actually... maybe that isn't a shadow? The door slams shut. Darkness. Silence. Then I hear the footsteps...

Aaliya Naqvi (12)
Kew House School, Brentford

Worried Wonders

The cold hit me. Walking through the woods was like feeling a shiver crawling up my back. Owls were hooting, *tu-whit-tu-whoo!* Crows called, always a bad sign. Feeling nervous I could hear my own heartbeat in my ears. It beat faster and faster when suddenly a breaking twig noise came from behind me. I turned around, nothing there... Growling all around. Wolves rose from the trees, they all started to chase me. Panting non-stop, getting slower after running so much. Paws gripped my clothes as I fell to the ground. All I heard was growling. Then no sound...

Anjali Gill
Kew House School, Brentford

THE INTRUDER

The night was dark as death, and in this foggy night a teenage girl was sitting on the sofa. Suddenly, she heard a noise coming from the window. There was a man holding a knife. Scared, the girl stayed still for a few seconds and then ran away. In a little while she stood up. Looking for the stranger, the girl saw bloody steps. Immediately she grasped the phone to call the police. The electricity went out. He was already in front of her. Nobody knows who is alive and who isn't. People say that everyone who went there was never seen again.

KREMENA KASABOVA (13)
Kew House School, Brentford

THE BEAST

Jacob was panting. The tremendous growling seemed to come closer to the tree which Jacob was behind. His legs were shaking, his lips trembling. He was frozen with fear. The growling would be sure to terrify anyone it went near. The crimson eyes glowed in the dark and its ragged black coat of fur enclosed the beast. In a flash Jacob's slim and lanky body made a dash for the gate. The muddy ground caused him to slip. The fear was evident in his eyes as he saw the wild beast approach him. Fear gripped his body.

BEN GINTY (13)
Kew House School, Brentford

At Night He Comes

Sleep beckoned, but was interrupted by a breeze crawling down my neck. An open window? No. My bedroom door creaked. I wanted to roll over but couldn't, sensing his dark eyes boring holes into my back. I started mouthing the words, 'Please leave,' over and over again, hugging my knees closer to my chest, but knew that he wouldn't. I tried to convince myself he wasn't there. For a moment things were still giving me hope. Then his icy hand touched my shoulder and once again filthy lips whispered things, enticing me to let him in.

Akerke Makhmud (18)
Kings School Oxford, Oxford

Elevator For The Deceased

Stepping into the hospital elevator, I greeted the woman next to me. She looked up and smiled. When the doors began to close I saw him. His face seemed familiar. Accusingly, he began to open his robe revealing black sutures across his chest. My sutures. My insides twisted and I gagged. Hastily, I took a step back and the elevator began to move. The woman turned to look at me. 'Tha-a-at was the man I operated on. His black wristband, it's for the deceased.'
The woman wasn't taken aback. Without fidgeting she lifted up her wrist. 'Something like this?'

Helen Chivadze (16)
Kings School Oxford, Oxford

GONE...

The distant sound of bombs attracted Raven. She crept cautiously behind the rickety bridge, desperate to stay hidden. Thick fog wove through the planks. Caught off guard, Raven didn't notice the figure emerging. An icy hand skimmed her shoulder. Raven swung a punch towards the figure, but it pulled out a sword and sliced her hand. The pain was immense. She screamed. Raven knew she had to run. But she couldn't move. The figure tried to cut her again but missed, as Raven was on the bridge. A plank of wood gave way and she vanished into the sea.

AMELIA MCGREGOR (11)
Lea Manor High School, Luton

THE DARK CREATURE

On a summer's evening, he was off to the News Station collecting the fresh batch of books for his comic store. The locals didn't like him; they say he's too happy, always walking somewhere, always... smiling.
As he carried the box of goods, he could feel the uneasiness of guilt. Like he'd just done something or he could have done something to change whatever he felt. But he was just collecting books... what could he have done wrong? That feeling struck him physically as suddenly a dark creature bit him. 'W-what?' James stuttered. Strangely, he could not move.

HARRY DOHERTY (15)
Lea Manor High School, Luton

The Overtime Nightmare

My car is shaking. All my hope has gone into this car that better not stop me. As I go on, more and more trees and bushes appear. Why did I have to work overtime? *Bang!* Not now, five miles left of jungle, now it stops. Voices in my head are telling me something. My head's spinning... screams, shouts, whispers. A rush of wind chills down my spine. Everything goes silent... No reception to call. No hope to rely on. I close my eyes, open them slowly and awake in a bed. Shivering, 'One of those dreams,' I say.

Mikhail Ali Ravjani (11)
Lea Manor High School, Luton

The Stuff Of Nightmares

I'm in a cave, surrounded by darkness, not knowing which way to go, scared. I take a left, or is it a right? I see something in the dark. I start to sweat; what is that? If I could see myself, I'd be sure I was pale. A set of blood-red eyes appear out of nothing. I freeze. I see it moving closer and closer and closer! A dagger appears. Any time soon, I'd stand no chance. The dagger is raised... I'm shaken. What?
'Come on Bob, time for breakfast!'
Oh, just a dream. I go downstairs to have breakfast.

Ben Yazzdi Parks (12)
Lea Manor High School, Luton

The Girl

One night a woman was alone in her house trying to get back to sleep after she had been woken up by loud wind banging on her window. Something didn't feel right. Suddenly the wind stopped and an ear-piercing scream came from her bathroom. She got out of bed and cautiously walked towards her bathroom. In a flash, the door slammed open and a girl with long brown hair, with dark eyes, dressed in a white dress appeared and stared her deep in the eyes. A shiver ran down her spine as she didn't know what had happened.

Daniella McIntosh (11)
Lea Manor High School, Luton

The Woman In Black

The look of terror on her face, her heart pounding. Everything was still. Suddenly, she heard the sound of something creeping up behind her. Turning around, she could see nothing apart from the crumbling gravestones.
'Hello?' she whispered, her voice bouncing from tree to tree.
With beads of sweat trickling down her forehead, she stumbled backwards, her clammy hands trying to find the edge of a gravestone. Her eyes adjusting to the darkness, a mysterious figure appeared before her. A woman, in a cloak, with a crooked walking stick. Sneakily, she drew something from her cloak and then came... Darkness.

Lily Pestell
Lea Manor High School, Luton

The Graveyard

The wind whipped at my tattered jacket sleeve. My thoughts blackened as I crept on through the abandoned graveyard. This was the only way out and I knew it. I ventured on, passing crumbling gravestones. Suddenly I heard a whisper, 'Come play with me...' Terrified, I slowly turned around. A girl wearing a white gown sat on a grave. Her thick black hair covered her face. 'Come and play with me,' she whispered. Her hands swept her hair out of her face. Her eyes were deep red, she smiled uncomfortably.
Was this the end? Or is it just the beginning...?

Kayleigh Greene (11)
Lea Manor High School, Luton

The Forest

It all started like this. Michael never listened to his parents. Today he was going to the forest, not any forest, a place where he might meet his end. The foolish, ignorant child ambled in cautiously. Little did he know that a monster was lurking in the pitch-black darkness. Suddenly, he heard eerie noises coming from behind the trees. Sweat trickled off his forehead as he gulped. A chill went down his spine as he screeched in horror. There was a hand on Michael's shoulder. As he turned around, an ugly, menacing monster grabbed him by the neck and... *drip, drip.*

Rayhan Ahmed
Lea Manor High School, Luton

Agnes

I threw my sister's disturbing doll, Agnes, into the dustbin before climbing into bed. I was so exhausted I slept almost instantly.
I abruptly woke up from squeaking and I realised my rocking chair was swinging back and forth. I gently twisted the seat around and my heart nearly skipped a beat. Agnes had a sinister smirk on her face.
'Come, play with me... forever,' her menacing voice demanded.
I crawled backwards on my bed, frantically trying to find some footing. The malicious doll crawled over me. Suddenly a blanket of jet-black fog enveloped me into darkness.

Lesley Ndjana (11)
Lea Manor High School, Luton

Do You Dare?

Taking small, steady steps towards the deserted house. Spooky black bats were hovering around me. Suddenly a fierce wind came through, breaking the doors apart. Entering the house, a dark silhouette was right in front of me. Loud footsteps sprinted from behind. I turned around. No one was there; the silhouette had vanished. My small hands started shaking and were unable to stop. Slowly creeping up the weightless stairs, a voice whispered into my ear, 'Do you dare?'
My heart thumping, I looked to my right, out of the corner of my eye. Fully turning my head, there it was staring...

Mahima Samiya (13)
Lea Manor High School, Luton

Help!

Running, it's all I was doing. Running away from whatever lurked between the trees. It was tall, slim and fast. I felt like every fibre of my body was shaking with fear... Then the loudest shriek pierced my eardrums. It sounded familiar. 'Mum?' I screamed. As I turned around, the most horrible sight. Dead bodies of everyone I knew. The man was gone but I was really scared now. I called everyone. They were okay. I was relieved. But then... I felt a cold breath on the back of my neck. I turned around and everything went black.

Andrew Russell-Hardiman (11)
Lea Manor High School, Luton

The Elevator

The lights flickered and the lift jerked awkwardly. The man next to me fell onto my shoulder and suddenly the elevator dropped and viciously stopped. People across from me looked alarmed, except one. A young girl cowered into her mother, who was pretending to be calm. I looked intently into a woman's eyes and started to notice something strange. Her eyes twitched and rolled around in her sockets. They became darker and darker until they were black. We stared in disbelief. Screaming and crying of the young girl filled the lift. Then there was blackness and one last piercing shriek!

Cerys Shaw (12)
Lea Manor High School, Luton

Halloween Night

Ruby was trick or treating for the first time with her new nanny. When they were going to the next house they saw a bunch of people near the abandoned graveyard, so Nanny went to see what was going on. In the crowd Ruby accidentally let go of Nanny's hand. The little girl was swept along in the crowd and crept through the police cordon. She was unseen. Ruby couldn't find the path back. She saw a lantern and went towards it. A policeman spotted her and caught her hand. The policeman's hand went through Ruby's small pale arm. Was she a ghost?

Skye Brosnan (11)
Lea Manor High School, Luton

The Anguished Father

My ears are red, my fingers are numb and I'm sitting on a cold hard bench made of gravel. The moon sits high above me in the clouds, glistening in the darkness, providing me with the only light I have. I am here in the graveyard to witness my father reincarnate. I set his corpse ablaze out of rage. His life is now nothing but an angered soul, a grim reaper coming for me. He is a devil in a black cape, carrying a scythe with his eyes on me. You cannot outrun the devil. Father now rests peacefully.

Foysol Ahmed (13)
Lea Manor High School, Luton

Machine Gun Madness

As the door swung open a mysterious figure entered. She had a walking stick. When she heard the creak of the door her walking stick turned into a machine gun! *Bang! Bang!* and she continued to shoot. The house had hundreds of bullet marks. As the little girl ran as fast as she could to get away she came to a dead end in the middle of the forest. The figure came closer and closer. She screamed, waiting for someone to hear. It got closer, it was slowly pulling out a piece of paper which said on it 'Come to me...!'

Hannah Watson (11)
Lea Manor High School, Luton

The Figure In The Fog

Through the foggy night, I could see a tall, deformed figure in the distance. My breath froze in the Arctic air. The trees swayed in the howling wind. Suddenly my phone vibrated. Signal! I rushed to reach for it, but before I could, there was a voice: 'You want to know where she is?' Laughter filled my ears.
I crouched onto the floor, covering my ears. Then screams filled the whole forest. 'Evie?' As I got my balance, frozen tears were running down my rosy, warm cheeks. The figure was beside me, its breath warming my face. I was frozen. Afraid.

Rebecca Grogan (13)
Lea Manor High School, Luton

I Haven't Thought Of One Yet

I'm scared, it's coming for me... Three nights ago I had a dream about a guy, fully dressed in a cloak, flipping a coin, over and over. It started at the bottom of the stairs and made it to the top. The next night it started at the top, making its way to my door. Still forever flipping the coin. Last night I woke up with it 3cm away from my face. I'm falling asleep now. Stay awake! I can't do it. The figure leans into my sight. The coin's gone. I can feel it in my throat. I'm choking.

Clare Lansfield (12)
Lea Manor High School, Luton

Doll House

Her eight-year-old heart pounded surprisingly as she felt the warmth of a small hand approaching her shoulder. The chaos in the dimly lit room escaped through her breath. 'Whoa...' her voice came slowly out of Frannie's stuttering mouth. The hand disappeared, a small girl, perhaps the same age as Frannie, flickered through her eyes.
'Come with me. Can we play?' the girl said, comfortably.
Frannie nodded, following her, in seconds appearing in a different room, different atmosphere. Frannie looked at the girl, her eyes turning to Frannie. She'd suffer, realising she was a doll inside a doll's house. 'Goodbye.'

Mai Blahuta (12)
Lea Manor High School, Luton

Goosebumps

Trembling, goosebumps running up my arms. We padded towards the outlawed hospital, it was full of dolls, all sorts of dolls. 'Oh my god, did they used to keep children in here?'
'This place is creepy, smells like something died in here!'
'I think we should get out of here!'
'What are you doing here Regina?'
She pulled the string of the doll and it repeatedly uttered, 'Follow me! End up like me!'
I found myself in a trance and a few days later I got creepy text messages after I came out of that place lost in fear.

Latifah Ali
Lea Manor High School, Luton

I Watched It

As my back arched, I knew that the cold blade had buried itself into my skin. I was left sitting against the abandoned library wall - helpless. The killer's next victim was Caleb. I watched a knife slice his throat so vigorously. He killed my friends randomly and with no known motive. The last to die was Lauren. She fought desperately but was inferior to the killer's strength and was driven out of the six-storey building to face her inevitable death. Then the killer left, leaving me to steal a final breath before I joined my friends in Heaven.

Chloe Stretton (13)
Lea Manor High School, Luton

Nightmare Horror Story

I sat there in vain hoping to get my revenge. She would pay! I spent every day of my life planning my revenge. Finally it was complete. *Bang!* A storm was creeping in, perfect weather. She came around, clueless, that night and had dinner. My plan was starting to take place. Little did she know that I had glued her down to her chair and she was about to have the fright of her life. I was supposed to make dinner but I was getting my laser prepared for tonight. I brought the laser out and she exclaimed, 'I'm your mother.'

Aliyah Iqbal (11)
Lea Manor High School, Luton

The Glass Room

As the door opened both rooms grew darker until a passageway appeared in the roof. Immediately, Jimmy decided to escape through it, but he didn't know how to get up high enough until he remembered the old rusty stepladder in the corridor which he had come from. So he put it on the crate from the corner and climbed out of the room. He was finally free and started to run towards the city in the distance, but he hit an invisible barrier. Jimmy stepped back, confused about what was happening. He fell over and went to sleep...

Dylan Joy (13)
Lea Manor High School, Luton

The Devil's Spawner

Once upon a time there was a monster. She had eight eyes. The shimmering sun blinded her so she shut six eyes. She went on to land and transformed into a human. She made friends with two girls. They did everything together. Until the two girls started to talk about boys and teen stuff. Every day they got more annoying. Then the monster transformed and opened all of her hideous eyes. She devoured both of them with a demonic smile.
'What happened to the monster?' asked Shelby.
Josie smiled, 'I am the monster, and you're next!'
Darkness covered the skies.

Rhianna John (11)
Lea Manor High School, Luton

The Never-Ending Street

I dawdled down the blackened street and suddenly stopped. Under the flickering lamppost was a ghostly black figure. I diverted my course and this time started to scamper. Every house around me was abandoned, boarded up windows and doors. No cars were in sight. I started to become distressed. I was moving faster than ever before, the street was never-ending. Suddenly my hurry came to a stop. I'd seen the same rusty deteriorated car ten times. I turned around steadily and the ghostly black figure was still there, under the same flickering lamppost. 'It's just a dream,' I whispered.

Dylan Vickery (13)
Lea Manor High School, Luton

The Vampire

As the little girl walked up the spooky steps the sign said 'Keep Out' but the little girl ignored it. The door creaked open. She walked in and looked around the house. The little girl walked up the steps. Every time she put her foot on the step it would creak. When she finally got up the steps she went into a room and saw a bloodthirsty vampire. The little girl screamed and ran into another room. She locked the door. 'Hopefully the bloodthirsty vampire doesn't get me,' she said. She unlocked the door to see him.

Maya Eleanor Brown (11)
Lea Manor High School, Luton

Trick Or Treat!

Shadows floated across the ground. Bob and Jeff walked towards the creepy mansion. It wasn't only haunted by cobwebs, but by ghosts and many other evil things. Jeff twisted the doorknob... Immediately, they were surrounded by ghosts, zombies, cats, witches and mummies. Horrified looks spread across their faces. Too terrified to run, they stood as still as they could. The monster approached. At first, Bob and Jeff had thought that they were illusions, but now no illusion was possible. Bob tugged Jeff with him and ran as fast as he could away from the creepy mansion. The teenagers sighed sadly.

Ryan Charlie Whittington (13)
Lea Manor High School, Luton

The Dark Knight

Lightning and thunder had masked the dark night sky. On the news Victor saw that there was going to be major traffic on the A18. Victor decided to take on one of the back routes to his house. A soft breeze hit Victor as he got nearer to the abandoned church. Victor's car suddenly jerked then broke down right in front of the cursed church he had chosen to enter. He saw a gloomy shadow out of the corner of his eye. He could hear the laughter of children. He had no idea what to do next...

Akshay Katechia (13)
Lea Manor High School, Luton

The Last Scream!

The door slammed shut. I was trapped. No way out. Could this be the end? My head was spinning round in circles. What was happening? 'Help!' I shouted, but it just died in the eerie room. Suddenly the floorboard creaked. The sound didn't leave my head. 'Hello?' I nervously turned around to see if anyone would answer. No answer. Before I knew it, I couldn't breathe. I couldn't see, hear or speak. I was senseless. I tried to scream. No use, all I could do now was pray and hope. I kept screaming. No use. Was that my last scream?

Ellie Sutton-Melrose (13)
Lea Manor High School, Luton

She's Coming...

His hand shook as he reached for his fork. Arthur lifted it to his mouth. The fog slithered through the open window. The light flickered. *I must not think of it, not of last night,* he thought to himself. But that night would be scarred in his mind forever. Suddenly his fork tumbled from his hand. As he crouched down there came the sound of his doorbell. Standing up, Arthur limped to his old, decrepit door. Gathering all his courage he swung it open. There she stood, still in her work clothes. She was here. She had come for him.

Annabel Cook (13)
Lea Manor High School, Luton

The Calling

This screech was higher pitched than the previous ones. Continuing down the cobbled walkway, I noticed that there were no signs of life, apart from one well kept patch of grass.
The giant door was of oak quality, yet felt like steel. Another screech. It came from inside the pantry.
A demonic creature stepped out, no eyes, no chest and no face. Its neck twisted. It declared 'We are the forgotten, we are the forgiven and we are the calling!' And with that the creature consumed the girl and crawled back to its hellish domain.
We are the calling.

Thomas Reuben Bottoms (13)
Lea Manor High School, Luton

The Dead Should Stay Dead

Fear and utter terror lurked within the village. Day after day the creature came. It awoke, lurking amongst the shadows, waiting for its next victim. Slash after slash he took many lives. Joseph was seven and was its latest victim, but it doesn't end there because he was buried in a cemetery to awaken him. However, his parents did not know he would never be the same. Joseph wasn't their precious, sweet little boy anymore as he sliced through his mother's throat with a large sharp knife. Legend states he was no longer human, he was the soulless Devil himself!

Kia-Jade Douglas (13)
Lea Manor High School, Luton

The Face In The Mist

The icy wind blows, it feels unnatural. I see a barn. I've got to go in. I'm on my own. I'm going in. An other-worldly mist of light floats by. It's weird, it goes straight through me. I don't like it, I run to the door but somehow it's locked from the outside. The light, it's there again, this time I can see what it is. The face of a child and a hand reaching out as if it's trying to grab me. 'Help!' I scream but nothing comes out. I try to run but I am stuck. Goodbye friends.

Leigh Terrance Wrigglesworth (13)
Lea Manor High School, Luton

The Hand That Turned The Corner

Turning the corner, *crunch,* the twigs snap. Sometimes I wonder if I'm the only one left. Snapping again, again. Every noise echoes through the galaxy. Each step creating more tension. The two hundred-year-old hand appears on the wall creaking like an old staircase. It's my time. All the preparation has come down to this. I've finally found my destiny. Slowly my skin peels away like a razor was tearing away at my limbs. I've got a choice, what will I choose: run or fight? Sometimes I feel like I'm the only one here. Alive!

Ryan Simmons (13)
Lea Manor High School, Luton

The Girl And The Shadow

Dark, isolated and cold. She sat while echoes of unwanted noises filled the room. Her mother had been missing for five years now and it was all she thought about. Outside, lightning struck while rain dashed down. She had never been in this position before. A shadow crept past her back and forth, trying to say something but couldn't. It came to a standstill. Eye to eye the girl and the shadow met. 'Argh!' Pin-drop silence. Who was it? We will never know!

Naiya Khetia (13)
Lea Manor High School, Luton

Forest Of The Dead

Suddenly I felt a shiver. All I had to do was walk through the forest to go to the shop. Right? As soon as I enter the forest I saw a shadowy figure. As I got closer I realised it was just a harmless old man with a cough. Something was weird though, he looked different. Then it hit me, he was a zombie! He must have been infected! In a flash fifteen zombies were chasing me! 'Help! Help!' I screeched. Out of nowhere a creepy house appeared. It was my only hope. I entered swiftly. Would I survive?

Shawn Denham (11)
Lea Manor High School, Luton

Footsteps

Her breath got hitched in her throat; booming footsteps were not far behind. *Boom!* Joselyn twisted around slowly to see nothing but fog. She didn't know why there was fog in her house. 'Hello?' she called out. Joselyn heard nothing but her echo. She tried again several times and got the same result: nothing. She tried one more time, however, this time a bristly hand touched her shoulder. Her feet allowed her to turn around and when she did a piercing scream exited her mouth.
Joselyn woke up drenched in her sweat. 'It was all a dream,' she whispered.

Natay Thompson (14)
Lea Manor High School, Luton

The Thing That Followed

'No, no, no, no!' I practically screeched at myself repeatedly, using all my strength to move my legs just a little bit quicker, away from that thing. Despite the ache encasing my whole body. I kept on. It couldn't end like this - me dead, in some isolated part of the woods. I heard the heavy flap of wings getting more pronounced and gave a cry of desperation and paused my supposed escape. My eyes darted around and I found a thick tree. I pressed my back to it and prayed. Then it was there, and it ended, just like that.

Casey Ronan (13)
Lea Manor High School, Luton

Alone And Helpless

Suddenly the aesthetic atmosphere darkened. Wolves howled, things looked as if they were to fall when the cold wind rushed through the trees, cracking the woods. I was alone, in the middle of nowhere, expecting someone to rescue me. I prayed. I heard men shouting from the distance, but I was hopeless. My legs stuck in some kind of trap. The feeling of fear got closer. I screamed in pain. Surprisingly a stranger, whose whole body was covered in blood, came forward and helped me out. He took me by the hand and smiled. My skin crawled. I was terrified beyond words.

Abdul Sami (15)
Lea Manor High School, Luton

The Abandoned Barn

The bitter cold wind sent an unsatisfying shiver up my icy spine. I was waiting outside the ancient, repugnant barn. We were filming a ghost documentary because the barn was supposed to be haunted. However, as usual she was inconveniently late so I decided to walk in myself... petrified, isolated in a gloomy evacuated room. The sudden creak of a loose floorboard made me regret the decision of coming in alone. The blood-curdling scream of my friend shrieked out my name. I rushed towards her. An impulsive hand wound around my neck, pulling me back...

Lily Massie (13)
Lea Manor High School, Luton

Three Hundred Years

The tall, dark-haired man walked past the mysterious house which had sat there for 300 years.
'La la la, la la la,' the mysterious house sang. Instead of running, the man walked in. He was known for not being scared of anything. There were rooms each side and stairs to the right with mould and ivy crawling round and round the staircase. There was fog running down the stairs. He took one step into the kitchen and a cold hand touched his shoulder. He screamed at the top of his lungs, waiting for footsteps.

Stephanie Butcher (11)
Lea Manor High School, Luton

HELL'S DOORS OF PUNISHMENT

One day a boy named Isaac was adventuring in his dad's basement when his dad gave him money to buy a toy. Singing songs, Isaac noticed piles of dead children with knives pierced through their heads. The poor child continued walking as rain burst into storms. Tears were coming from his eyes as he ran quickly through the forest. Turning in fear he saw a black figure with blood-covered horns. Isaac tried to outrun him and hide but he was almost stabbed. Managing to turn to the path to his house, he found his blood-covered dad, dead!

SCOTT TERENCE HERBERT (11)
Lea Manor High School, Luton

THE HORROR BIN

The fog started creeping in as Tom looked at the stove that didn't work properly. It started making noises and people were whispering in their heads saying, 'Run but you can't hide,' in a faint voice. Tom screamed and Martin bellowed, 'We're not scared.'
A few minutes later Tom and Martin heard a noise in the hallway. There it went again, but much closer. *Boom! Crash!* went the thunder outside. Tom decided to investigate. In the evening Martin saw a little doll on the floor, he picked it up and the head moved from good to bad. It looked evil...

MIKAEL EDUBATEY (12)
Lea Manor High School, Luton

Dragon Attack

A curled, hideous and sleeping moody dragon, the colour of bright dazzling gold coin, around her neck is a letter titled Stormfly! An enormous lightning bolt filled with poison attacks another victim nearly every second. The howling and the fearsome, frightening dragon is approaching the woods. Twenty unspeakable people crowded what we saw as an incredible dark beast soaring through the treetops. Being furious with rage that is unbeatable, its cold-blooded red and black gruesome body was as big as a skyscraper. Bloodsucking creatures that like to feed on blood-filled adrenaline.

Abdul Kabir (11)
Lea Manor High School, Luton

In The Darkness

'James?' I called, swinging the torch frantically around the pitch-black church. I heard a movement behind me and turned around quickly. The torch faded, now emitting a very dim light. I could just make out a figure standing on one side of the room. 'James?' I called, moving towards the figure. As I drew closer I noticed a small pair of red eyes staring emotionlessly at me. I stopped dead in my tracks, body tensing. I could feel some kind of abnormal presence behind me. I felt a cold breath on my neck. My voice shook with fear. 'James?'

Delilah Fulton (13)
Mayville High School, Southsea

UNTITLED

It was a long, cold winter, one that rains every day. Not only had it been a long, cold winter for Ted, but also a long, hard day at work. At last he was home. Finally alone. At last he was out of the rain and wind. Finally alone. As he opened the front door, carefully not letting too much rain in, Ted found himself in complete darkness, although he was sure he remembered to leave the hallway light on. Even more strangely, Ted heard a clanging noise from upstairs. He got the sense that he was no longer alone.

JEMIMA PARKYN (14)
Mayville High School, Southsea

UNTITLED

I was walking home. It was windy so my hair whipped my face. But it was dark and cold. My steps quickened as a car with bright headlights zoomed past me into the mist. That's when I saw them, a group all running towards me. I began to run. Then I remembered the alley... I sprinted down it and hid in the corner, trying to keep my breathing steady as the sound of footsteps came closer and closer. I held my breath as the torch shone onto me.

CHARLOTTE WEBB
Mayville High School, Southsea

Silhouette

A cold, dark night is never a good sign. It's even worse when the street lights have lost power and you're the only one walking down the road at midnight. Georgia was walking quicker than she normally would because it was so late and she knew her parents were going to punish her for missing her curfew. She heard someone following her. She felt them getting closer. Then, it was as if they were right behind her. The silhouette was just visible in the puddle in front of her. Georgia stopped. She never returned home on that cold, dark night.

Emily Annice Devonshire (14)
Mayville High School, Southsea

Untitled

Standing alone, the girl stood on the rotten jetty, watching waves lap beneath her and reaching out like claws trying to pull her into the murky depths of the ocean. Occasionally, a seagull would let out a harsh shriek as if trying to warn her of the dangers which lurked below the surface.

Looking out to sea, the girl suddenly felt the temperature drop and thick dense sea fog rolled off the waves. Peering through the fog, she could see a shadow approaching from beneath the waves. It disappeared! Then, she felt something slimy grab her by the ankle.

Emily Sale
Mayville High School, Southsea

THE BOY IN THE CORNER

It dawned on them, what was that noise over there in the corner? There it was again! It could be the ghost the team were looking for. Crying, weeping, footsteps, it had all been reported, that's why the ghost catchers were there. It felt like the walls were whispering, 'The boy, the boy.' It was as silent as death. Uncomfortable feelings flowing through them. The shadows were dancing all over the place. What was going to happen next? They couldn't question the fact that the boy in the corner was real and there was no way he was leaving soon.

CHARLOTTE NEAL (11)
Mount St Mary's College, Sheffield

THE VAMPYRE HUNTER

In the darkened chapel I stood armed with a wooden stake, a hammer, a gun with silver bullets and finally an axe. I was there to fight her, the mistress of the Devil, the vampyre. I crept down into the crypts. I opened her coffin and there she was. I went to strike her heart, but first I looked round to make sure I wasn't in danger. I looked back and she was gone! She grabbed me! I tried to shoot her but missed. She then ripped out my heart. I fell to the floor. Dead. Hours later I awoke...

ISAAC TETLEY (13)
Mount St Mary's College, Sheffield

Mama

'I am not as great a woman as I thought. I am not as strong as you perceive me to be. And I am sorry. I am proud of you, so proud. I love...' Mama's ramblings were cut short as the connection went dead.
A body landed on the ground outside the phone booth. Mama. Her splattered remains filled my eyes and the crunch of her bones rang in my ears before the shadows of the night enveloped me. Pain shot through my head. I landed on the ground next to her corpse.
'Yes ma'am, I assure you, it's done.'

Ada Kalu (17)
Mount St Mary's College, Sheffield

The Strange New Town

I woke up to the sound of thunder. I was in my mum's car driving to our new town. I looked outside the car window to see grim, grey skies. in the distance beyond, I saw a zombie look-alike.
We eventually got to our new town, it was pitch black, black as coal.
My spine was chilling, I knew something wasn't right about this.
As we stepped into our house I heard a bang in a closet. I opened the door and a doll fell on me. I got scared because of it and my mum was never found.

Gerard John White (13)
Salford City Academy, Manchester

Untitled

A normal winter's day, a boy was watching a movie, he was called Peter. Peter's film was called Ghost! A few minutes into the film the ghastly ghost jumped out of the TV! As it crawled towards him slowly he dashed upstairs and shouted for his mum.
She replied, 'What are you doing?'
Peter was about to reply but was stopped in his tracks by the sight of a dark shadow.

Ramiar Shafie
Salford City Academy, Manchester

The Airport Toilet Of Doom

It was a cloudy Saturday night as the clock struck nine. Jaimie, Oliver, Amy and Jimmy were stood there, going through airport security when they noticed a dilapidated toilet. Oliver needed the toilet so he went inside it and noticed the toilet was abandoned because there was a dead WHSmith's worker on the floor, blood dripping from their head. As Oliver was about to run out, an ancient ghost drifted toward him, knocking him out. When it struck midnight, the Connor family boarded the plane, thinking Oliver was dead. They had to get away.

Oliver Lefley
Salford City Academy, Manchester

Shadows Of Evil

It was a dull yet peaceful night but Patricia was pacing furiously! The thing chasing her, leaping left and right! 'Patricia, where are you?' cried her friends! Patricia heard them through the mountains but she didn't have the strength to shout back. Patricia paused at a dead end and she collapsed to the ground!
'Where am I?' Patricia shouted with all her energy! Patricia looked with anger as a mysterious figure emerged from the dark. 'Who are you? What do you want? You have an option!' cried the man,
'Wait... Dad, is that you there?'

Hassam Shahid
Salford City Academy, Manchester

Night

It was dark, gloomy, petrifying. My spine was shivering. Me and my friend were outside a horrifying house. It was black, pitch-black. It was silent, the sky had a full moon, owls howled. Me and my friend grabbed each other's hand and gulped. We stumbled up to the dilapidated house. I felt like I was going to pass out. Wind, heavy wind, started to blow on our faces. I felt my friend letting go of my hand, she was gone. I was alone. 'Help!'

Molly Jayne Burtonwood
Salford City Academy, Manchester

UNTITLED

One day I was on a plane to somewhere warm, everyone was talking to each other then suddenly something happened... The plane was flying down so fast, like a comet. Lots of people were screaming and shouting to save their children. Someone or something was laughing that we were going to die, he was sat at the back laughing then a big bang happened... We crashed.
I woke to a spooky black bloom, some helicopters found the plane and I was passed out. I was the only person who lived and I don't know why.

JORDAN KURTZ (14)
Salford City Academy, Manchester

UNTITLED

I was woken up by the screeching, horrible noise of a half-man, half-zombie grinding his razor-sharp claws against the pointed edged, rough surface of the cleaver. I tried to get up to run. However, I realised that there was a stiff, rough rope clutching my body together. The zombie was coming towards me with his ugly, ragged, horrific nails full of blood. His greasy long hair was as long as him. My heart was beating as fast as a drum. I thought it was over.

ABDULQADER ABDULLA
Salford City Academy, Manchester

Untitled

I woke up feeling terrible. I wished I were dead. I opened my eyes, I wondered where I was. I was in a blacked-out and bleak house, freezing, curled up in a bed. All of a sudden a piece of wood fell to the floor and made a big bang. You could hear the spiders crawling round the room, eating ants and flies. Then I heard a voice. I hid under the bed. This creature leapt out of the shadows growling, blood coming from its mouth. It bit my living flesh. 'Argh!' I screamed. I thought, *this is it!*

Anees Hamad
Salford City Academy, Manchester

Untitled

It was a dark, scary night in the hollow, empty streets of London. Jim and Bob were wandering. Bob saw in the distance a hooded figure flying into this abandoned house called The House of the Weeping Angel.

Jim turned to look and he didn't see anything. Jim said, 'Stop over-reacting!'

But then Bob ran to the house. Searching everywhere for this flying figure but there was nobody. Then he heard a noise so Bob ran up the creepy stairs to see the figure in the corner. He shouted, 'What are you doing here?'

The figure turned to face Bob...

Blake Smith
Salford City Academy, Manchester

Untitled

I was driving down a long, bumpy road in my matte black car and out of the corner of my eye I could see a dilapidated, abandoned house which was the size of ten football pitches. I slowly got out of my car and crept through the rusty fence to enter the ancient, haunted house.
I opened the door to see a long hallway with a large figure emerging from the distance. I turned around to run but the door shut in my face. I fell through the dusty, wooden planks breaking all my bones and screaming for help.

Acer Kennedy
Salford City Academy, Manchester

Mummy And The Kid

It was a dark night. There was a sandstorm brewing and Bob's dad was in the pyramid. Bob decided to go into the pyramid to see his dad. In there was a ring with a black diamond. He tried to take the ring off but he couldn't. He then suddenly started to see the past before his eyes. He started to dream of a mummy that killed a man. He got scared and started to hear noises. Had touching the ring released dead spirits?

Mitchell Cherepovski
Salford City Academy, Manchester

The Zombie And His Human Kid

It was a dark, foggy, cold night in the graveyard where Joe goes to visit his father who died. This was quite recent.
During the visit, Joe became very scared because he saw a hand pop out of the ground but he did not move because he was frightened. The hand was like that of a zombie.
Suddenly, he heard his father's voice, which made him tremble with fear. The hand started to move. He thought the hand was going to grab him and kill him, but it remembered... he was his son.

McKenzie Mercer
Salford City Academy, Manchester

The Scary Forest

It was a dark, scary night in the scary forest and there was a ghost that jumped out at people. It also looked at people through the trees and this frightened them!
The ghost went back to the trees, walking off and starting to haunt people. Then the ghost rushed behind people and touched them. They trembled and started to feel scared. There were eyes in the distance. Footsteps and door slamming could be heard.
The ghost sorted it out by smiling at people and talking to them. They decided to have a dance and a tea party.

Leah Jade Morris (14)
Salford City Academy, Manchester

Murder In The Morgue

I felt my heart pound. I was desperately lost. *How did I get here?* I glanced at my hands, they were stained with blood... *what did I do?* It was cold and draughty. A familiarly blood-chilling smell washed up my nostrils... I soon realised why... On metal slabs, sheets covered decaying bodies. I recoiled. I ran for the door - locked! The old light hanging from the flaking ceiling slowly flickered. Terrified, I screamed with torment. Bloody handprints were smeared against the wall, bursts of memory erupted through my mind... *What have I done?* The covered corpse slowly shifted. I screamed.

Helena Grant (11)
Silcoates School, Wakefield

Dark Figure

Lightning struck the trees as the whistling wind shook them violently. The rain came crashing down. *Bang! Bang! Bang!* There was a knock at the door. Meg went to answer it, but no one was there. Entering the kitchen, suddenly hearing a loud noise. She peeked her head around the door, the television - on! But how? *Bang!* There it was again. Meg stood, keeping her eye on the door. It vibrated the window, the frame, everything. She checked again, no one was there. Meg went upstairs, but a dark figure blocked her path. It reached out to grab her neck...

Taylah Malpass (12)
Silcoates School, Wakefield

The Graveyard

In the dead of night, under the light of the bloodstained super moon lay an abandoned graveyard. Inside, half-crumbling and sunken gravestones stood. On the twelfth hour of the twelfth day of the twelfth month of the twelfth year, the spirits came out to play. As the clock chimed twelve, mossy gravestones started to shake. A weird white mist came closer and closer. This funny fog had an unusual shape because it had wings on each side, a face and no legs. Ted realised that it wasn't fog, it was a spirit.

Edward Nutter
Silcoates School, Wakefield

Terror In Tescos

I was just driving down to the local supermarket to collect some supplies for the party I was planning for a friend. Soft drinks, crisps, paper plates, napkins, plastic cups, cake. There was so much to remember. My brain was full. I was concentrating so hard on getting everything I didn't notice how quiet the supermarket had become. As I was approaching the checkout I heard a distant slamming of a door. I was locked in. Then all of a sudden the lights started flickering on and off. I heard a faint voice of a child: 'I am watching you.'

Max Brocklesby (11)
Silcoates School, Wakefield

The Mist

Mist crept through a shrubby graveyard upon a moorland. Sherry could hear her heart pounding rapidly, her colossal feet squelched on the moist grey grass. Someone was watching her. She ducked low, hiding as her heart began to increase in speed. The dead trees, grey and dull, began to move slowly forward, side to side as a thick stench of rotting flesh flowed everywhere within the disused graveyard. Below her knees was a dozen pairs of footprints. Sherry followed the footprints. She stopped where the footprints ended. A cold bony hand pulled her into a hollow where she disappeared.

Harry Cooper (12)
Silcoates School, Wakefield

The Abandoned Maze

There in the maze with gnarled trees and bushes everywhere, cracked stones, no light, completely dark, no signal, so don't try calling for help. You are all alone. Statues staring into your face, the shadows following you everywhere you go. No escape. Cobbled walls that have nails sticking out that will viciously attack you and also the cobbled walls have rigid edges. Don't even attempt running because if you hit into those walls once - lights out for you. This maze will force you to have nightmares as long as it takes to set up a laptop that's never been used.

Nathan Oliver Wood (11)
Silcoates School, Wakefield

Walk To Gran's

All we had to do was walk through the graveyard (which still spooked me out from time to time) to get to my gran's house to give her the weekly food, fresh from the supermarket. I normally go with my little brother but I'd come straight from school so I brought some friends, Ben and Dan. The wind was shocking, it was whistling like it had never whistled before and the rain was bouncing down like a lion. Something was not right, the gravestones had moved one centimetre to the right because the flowers had moved...

James Robinson (12)
Silcoates School, Wakefield

Untitled

Five regular contestants marched through a mind-tricking maze to get the shiniest trophy in the world. When the race started, I ran as quick as I could but its wobbly path and hostile trees and branches growing from the walls made me feel a bit anxious, so I walked. The place itself was an old crumbling castle with a large and tricky maze under it. It was starting to creep me out but when I got to the trophy, I heard something.

Martin Marshall (11)
Silcoates School, Wakefield

Snow White And The Seven Devils

Strolling happily through the alluring, vivid forest, I approached a little house in front of my eyes. I walked into nothing, just a bare old room apart from seven little beds. I had a wander around to find an eagle trapped in a cage. I was not sure what to do. Suddenly, I heard a knock at the door then hid behind a plank of wood. The stairs creaked as something came towards me. My mind was lost. There stood seven little creatures. They lifted up their hands and there were guns sat in their palms. That meant death...

Chloe Newsome (11)
Silcoates School, Wakefield

Stranded

In the pounding rain, I approached the rusty iron gate. Cautiously I pushed the gate open, an eerie creak followed. Shuddering, I entered this nightmare. Decaying graves and tombs surrounded me like police arresting a dangerous criminal. I crept towards a battered wooden bench and took a seat. Suddenly, I lost the feeling in all my limbs. No matter how hard I tried I couldn't move an inch. I was stranded in an abandoned graveyard! Then in the misty distance a figure in black robes began to walk in my direction. When within a metre, the figure spoke. 'Hello boy...'

Josh Sheppard (11)
Silcoates School, Wakefield

'Grave' Danger

The moon's light crept upon the fragile gravestones as Will, the sapphire-eyed child, limped through the sludgy graveyard. He could see the pale translucent spirits guiding him to their abandoned gravestones. They said it was to purify their souls but Will knew it was to get into their previous bodies. Will knew for them to get life, they needed energy. While he was walking he met an eccentric soul, Pedro. Pedro reached out for Will's soul chain and tugged on it. Will screeched until he had no voice. Pedro started absorbing the chain's link. Will flopped to the ground, cold...

Kiran Sebastian Thachankary (12)
Silcoates School, Wakefield

The House

Halloween in the fiery stone towering structure. I looked up, I saw the huge brass knockers on the solid oak doors. My coffee filled eyes drifted sideways to the marble scraped pillars. I knew this wasn't any ordinary house. Creeping forward in trembling fear I noticed was crimson blood on the sides of the freezing doorknob. There was a note and it said 'Do not enter!'
In curiosity Tom shoved the oak door and gasped...

George Heptinstall (12)
Silcoates School, Wakefield

Destination

Rain hammered down as lightning struck the country lane. Slowly, the fuel meter was going down. He should've arrived at his destination now. He was starting to grow uneasy. A bolt of lightning struck straight in front of the car. He smashed down on the brakes and the car screeched to a halt. Lightning struck again. Out of the corner of his eye he saw a silhouette of a figure. Again it struck. It was advancing. This was too much. He frantically bailed out of the car and sprinted down the lane. He fell. He let the darkness swallow him...

Adam Samuel Wells (12)
Silcoates School, Wakefield

It's Just A Parcel...

Grins filled our faces, our bags crammed with sweets, we were nearly at our last destination. However, this house wasn't like the rest we scavenged from. Deserted. Ancient. Eyes wide open, I surveyed: windows, which were shattered into a million pieces; grass as deceased as our great grandparents; gas lamp, too old to still be working. There is something about this house that makes my heart thump so hard in my chest, that makes a shiver run down my spine... I placed my hand onto the ice-cold metal gate. Was I ready for what was inside? Just a parcel...

Katie Walker (12)
Silcoates School, Wakefield

Werewolf

I scrambled backwards as a high, animal scream of pain rang through the forest. Heart pounding in my chest, I peered through the darkness - a furry, bulky monster stood by a tree in the distance. Then all of a sudden it arched its back and pounced towards me, howling and screaming. I attempted to move but there was nothing I could do as the werewolf hit me like a truck and sank its fangs into my neck.

Isabel Eve Hodson (12)
Silcoates School, Wakefield

The Old Graveyard

In the dead of night, under the light of the bloodstained super moon, lay an abandoned graveyard where half-sunken, crumbling gravestones stood. Suddenly the old clock tower chimed. Amelia had an idea of how to escape. Cold, wet rain dripped off her grazed body. Amelia began to regret coming here. Was it a dare? Joshua was wandering around, bewildered and forlorn. Amelia knew the only way to escape was to collect the ectoplasm and add some acid and pour it onto the ghosts, which they did as a team.
When they did they heard: 'Hello.'
'Mum!'

Anna-Mai Lawrie (11)
Silcoates School, Wakefield

THE FIGURE

Darkness surrounded her. Once finished locking up, she would be free to go home. The light flickered on and off, on and off. Claire looked up at the constant flickering light. She caught a glimpse of a figure with a pure white blanket covering its mysterious body. Claire became scared, she was in a warehouse on her own! She grabbed the keys and fumbled for the right one, she took it, forced it into the lock, but it wouldn't turn. Something was wrong. The light went out. Suddenly it switched back on. The figure was now in front of her, watching...

THOMAS WALKER (12)
Silcoates School, Wakefield

A STRANGE CHRISTMAS

The best day of the year for most but Tom. One hour before the celebration begins, Tom finds himself in a lonely, desolate graveyard. Wrinkled and unwanted flowers lay next to gravestones. Tilted, crooked and cracked, the gravestones were tightly packed together like unbrushed teeth. Fading names and chipped edges, the village of gravestones surrounded him. Tom felt a warm breath on his neck. Was someone stalking him? Looking for their next victim? A breeze quickly rushed past as well as a strange, mysterious, spooky, frightening sound of footsteps approaching. Would he get out of there in time for Christmas?

CHARLOTTE I'ANSON (11)
Silcoates School, Wakefield

The Old Mill

Footsteps echoed around the old mill. Jake, Alex and I had only come in here to escape the storm, but now I couldn't find them. Rain thundered down on the windows. 'Guys?' I called. No answer. *Bang!* A machine fell to the floor. I began to walk faster. *Where are they?* Suddenly behind me machines began to fall, the sharp edges pointing at me. I began to run but the floor was slippery. With every step I nearly fell. They started to fall faster. *Are they chasing me?* I fell. My ankle began to throb. I stood up. *Bang!*

Jennifer Noble (12)
Silcoates School, Wakefield

The Phone Call

Ronald turned on the TV. He saw that they were still going on about the serial killer that had recently escaped from prison, Dr Lolly Pop. Suddenly, the phone went off. Little did he know that the call would result in a tragedy. He heard a slow breathing sound. 'Hello,' Ronald said.
'Hello Ron,' replied a high-pitched voice.
'Who is this?'
'An old friend,' said the man.
'I do not want any trouble.'
'You know your wife needs to be more careful with her knives.'
Suddenly a blood-curdling scream came from the kitchen.
'Stacy, no!' Ron horrifyingly yelled.

Felix Massouras (12)
Silcoates School, Wakefield

Nightmares

Darkness. That's all it was, nothingness. Slowly creeping up was a light, a blinding light like the sun. It dimmed and left behind a figure, it was staring. Alice felt its hypnotising glare pierce her eyes. What's this figure? Alice decided to have a closer look. It was wearing a nightie just like hers, however, the figure's had something different, it was blood-stained. Alice tried to move, to leave this horror but she couldn't, paralysed. Her blonde, long hair knotted and messy. The figure got closer, becoming more visible though more scary. Alice screamed a blood-curdling scream.

Emily Verinder (11)
Silcoates School, Wakefield

The Church

The rain fell under the blood moon. The church was old and worn down. Mark looked around for the exit. He ran as fast as he could. Suddenly he stopped and shuddered. Something cold and fleshy grabbed his leg. The wet earth was sucking him in. Mark struggled to get out but it kept sucking him in.

'You belong with us, in the grave!' a raspy voice slowly said.

'Nooo, what have I done?' Mark screamed. He saw a figure wandering in the darkness. 'Help!' he screamed.

The figure turned around. He came closer. Red eyes beamed at Mark...

Jack Slaski (11)
Silcoates School, Wakefield

Untitled

In the countryside there was a house. Parents gone, nobody home. Running towards the phone, hoping it's college. 'Welcome to Minister College, we have received...' the phone cut off. Everything seemed normal a minute ago, now what? Emma's heart beating as fast as a hummingbird's wings. Pacing into the lounge where the TV had blurred lines all over it. Eyes bloodshot, turning towards the radio but only crackling music came out. 'Hello from the other side.'
Emma fell onto the sofa, she only wanted to receive something. Until the key clicked in the door, nobody was back till later.

Lucy Brereton (12)
Silcoates School, Wakefield

Forget

India's purple hair was strewn across her face, the memory etched in her mind. Running, running through the forest, trying to discover the place of her haunting childhood playground. It was dark, the shadows of trees surrounded her... 'Please come down!'
'No!' Tabby jumped and landed gracefully on the branch below. It snapped, sending Tabby plummeting towards the rocky ground... India tripped, the rain glossed her blood-ridden knee. She lay there, sobbing. The memory of her sister dying was too much to handle. India was weak, giving up almost. Suddenly, bony hands pulled her back, into darkness.

Hannah Tindall-Miller (11)
Silcoates School, Wakefield

Trick Or Treating

It was trick or treating. The day Cindy would meet up with her friend and go around to every house in the state, asking for sweets. Cindy and Emma had vast amounts of sweets. They came across an old abandoned house with smashed roof tiles. A thought etched through their minds, wanting to have a peek through the abandoned house. They walked carefully through the rusty, crumbling graveyard. The sound of footsteps crept up behind Emma and Cindy. Emma jumped up to Cindy but they fell to the ground. The feeling of crumbling stone crept in. It was the end...

Hanna Bhatt (11)
Silcoates School, Wakefield

Pegasus Vs Unicorn

They were coming. I curled up in a ball, hoping for some kind of magic to happen. It wasn't going to happen, I was stranded. The dust I was curled up in tasted unfamiliar, it tasted a bit like rainbow pellets. It made me dazzle. I had already turned into a unicorn with my special powers. Nothing could stop me. I extended my horn. Nothing could stop me. Out of nowhere a pegasus appeared and bit my leg off. I was doomed. My rainbow dust was scattered along the floor. I was dead.

Connor Brady (12)
Silcoates School, Wakefield

The Lost Boy And Girl

The rusty gate creaked open. Katie and Adam were retrieving their ball. They walked through the garden, it was covered with broken bricks and smashed tiles. There was a sudden bang! In fright they ran into the old house. When Katie opened the door the light flickered. Adam softly closed the door, they both crept up the old creaky stairs and walked into the room on the left. There was a wardrobe with someone in it. They whispered, 'Hello.'
From the other side, 'Come.' The mysterious figure then popped out of the wardrobe and shouted, 'Surprise little kids!'

Jake Donson (11)
Silcoates School, Wakefield

The Dead Flower

Grace looked around. The beautiful flowers shimmered in the sun, except for one. It was grey and shrivelled. She picked it. Suddenly she felt the ground crumble. She was sucked under.
'The future is dark. Are you willing to give something to save it?' said a cold voice.
'Yes, whatever I must do.' As Grace said this a small light came out from the darkness. 'Touch this and it will restore the balance.'
Grace touched the orb of light and felt it draining the life out of her. She fell to the ground and became one with the earth.

Emily Bagshaw
Silcoates School, Wakefield

The Hand Of Numbness

Big Ben strikes twelve. A shiver runs up my spine. It feels like the whole universe has been put under a spell of silence. A deadly spell of silence. The blanket of darkness has surrounded me, like it's protecting me... A piercing ringing but at the same time screaming has suddenly begun. A rapid tapping noise has built up the volume and the wind is calling out to someone, like it's asking for help. My oven timer is going off. It's supposed to be broken... I turn it off. Someone taps me on the shoulder. My whole body goes numb.

Kate Bass (12)
Silcoates School, Wakefield

Trapped!

Crackling from the old radio made Lottie's heart stop beating. These few seconds caused confusion in the world, no one, no one at all. Everything was unnaturally still. *Bang!* Out of nowhere there was a spine-chilling noise,the door, the evil door which attempted to trap her, alone and with no escape. Her house that she thought she knew and trusted actually was one of those mean bullies that pick on you in the playground. A sense of claustrophobia suffocating her with every inch of its strength. She felt the most afraid she had ever felt in her life... She was trapped!

Charlotte Westmoreland-Smith (12)
Silcoates School, Wakefield

Blood Message

The scream shattering the silence. Blood gushing from the door, opposite my questioning glare. Trailing blood seems to stop dead at my feet, deep crimson. Spiteful glares of the growing crowd pierce my eyes believing I had something to do with the blood-curdling scream. Suddenly the door creaks half open. A finger creeps around the door frame followed by a blacked out eye. They have no place of coming. Appearing from nowhere, no skin, no body. The door slammed as a male from the crowd reached towards it. The blood disappearing with it, leaving nothing but an unread note...

Freja Wilson (11)
Silcoates School, Wakefield

No!

No, I will not go. The spirits may howl and risk everything to get close to me. But, no! They cry my name at dusk and wake me at dawn. But, no, I will not go. I'm trapped like a beast in a cage; alone, alone as can be. But, no! Threatened within my own territory: the scratch marks on my walls, the constant banging on the door and screeching at night. However, the thing that sickens me the most is knowing that they want to take me somewhere. Somewhere only devils go. But, no, I will not go... No!

Georgina Wolff
Silcoates School, Wakefield

This Night Shall Be Your Last

One night just like this one. A complete psychopath clown laughing to the storm above. He's in your school, he's in your home, he's killing your family. He's in your room. He's next to you. You can feel your spine getting cold, a knife by your neck. You turn to face a merciless clown showing no life in his eyes but then he says, surprisingly, 'See you in Hell.'
You hesitate for a while, not taking your eyes off him. The knife gets deeper into your flesh. Then he tears your heart out. 'This is the end,' he says smugly.

Charlie Holmes (11)
Silcoates School, Wakefield

Escaped

It came out of nowhere, I was pushed face down to the floor. I heard a crackle but when I tried to get up I was pushed back down. Whatever pushed me was very strong, I was struggling to get away. I couldn't move. The wind was powerful and loud, but the sound of a howl beat the wind's sound. I could hear footsteps, but that was all, until there was screaming. Not just from one person but from loads of people. Eventually I escaped, all I wanted to do was run away but I was very lost!

Poppy Roberts
Silcoates School, Wakefield

Tonight Was The Night!

Trees quivered in the nightly gale, mist wove its way through the damp fusty tombstones, the moon flickered through the towering trees. No one was there besides the six teenage girls, wandering hopelessly through the blood-curdling, bitterly cold, unilluminated woods: Hope, Sasha, Alex, Emma, Annabelle and Mac. Creatures of the night examined the six girls, baring their fangs at them. A grim screech came from behind them, shadowy figures rippled into the air. Tonight was the night... they all died! One by one the silhouette snatched all of the girls, leaving nothing but their purses in the dead of night!

Phoebe Smith (12)
Silcoates School, Wakefield

Cabin On The Lakeside

It was pitch-black and stormy. I woke up, my friend was awake too then we heard three knocks. My friend said, 'Hello?'
Suddenly the door melted. Then he said, 'I'm in the cabin.'
Everyone else in my room suddenly got up and said in time, 'Time to die!'
Before I knew it, the pale and wrinkly people disintegrated in front of my eyes. Then before my eyes stood a vampire. Scum! A cold-blooded fiend. He clasped my neck, piercing the skin. I let out a yell that echoed on and on! I am now a vampire!

Allister Isaac-Sheard (11)
Silcoates School, Wakefield

My Death Bed

I was in bed when I heard a spine-chilling bang! Then the stairs creaked. *Thud! Thud!* It was getting louder. I hid under the covers. It felt like I would have a panic attack. My door creaked open. 'Leave me alone!' I screamed. A cold hand grabbed my shoulder. *Bang!* I was hit on the head. The last thing I saw was a quilt of stars flashing above me. When I woke up, I found myself dangling over a pool of lava. The rope snapped. I fell to my doom! The pain was excruciating.

Jake Darnill (11)
Silcoates School, Wakefield

'A'

I walked into the deserted school, not knowing what would happen. Then there was a creak... 'Hello?' I whispered cautiously. 'Is anyone there?' Another sudden noise came! I ran into one of the dark rooms, it was creepy but it had to do. I pushed a heavy desk towards the door, when I realised I was being followed! The desk was in place, but behind the door, was a figure in a black hoodie! I turned around - eyes shut - the urge to open them defeated me. On the mirror before me were the words: 'You won't get out alive.' 'A'...

Charlotte George (11)
Silcoates School, Wakefield

House Of Horror

I walked up to the house. I was about to open the door, then all of a sudden I heard a girl screaming and the door opened, opened all by itself. I ran but I couldn't. Someone grabbed me or worse still - something. I turned around. There was nothing there. Strangely I walked into the house, my brain was saying, 'What are you doing? Turn around.' But I just kept going. Inside the house there was nothing apart from a table with a gun on it. I picked it up and *bang!* That was that, my whole life ended forever.

Sophie Brightman (12)
Silcoates School, Wakefield

Smile

Blackness, that's all I could see. I felt the hairs stand up on the back of my neck. A chill ran down my spine. I felt like I was standing in some warm water. A flicker of flame illuminated the room from a small candle holder. Now I know why I felt like I was in hot water. I was kneeling in a chamber and a lake of fresh blood. There were arms and legs still twitching. I looked down. To my horror a head was floating on the red surface. The head was a fixed, evil, deathly, devilish smile.

Jessica Allott (11)
Silcoates School, Wakefield

DOOM!

Knock, knock, knock went the door. A shadow lurked behind it. I jumped up with a chill as a spider ran across the floor. I opened the door and stepped onto the coffin-like step. I peered around seeing nothing but my own shadow. Turning back into the house I heard another knock. This time there was no shadow, but a big claw mark on the door. Whatever was happening outside was now inside. 'Boo!' 'Argh!' There was nothing there except 'You are doomed!' written on the door in mud. Note this, we never saw the man again.

WILLIAM SENIOR (11)
Silcoates School, Wakefield

WARD 34

Suddenly I awake. Where am I? it looks like a hospital! I cautiously swing my legs over the edge of the bed. Gradually I stand upright. I start to walk down a long, cold, stark corridor towards a bright light escaping through the edges of a door. Nurses are rushing around. 'Excuse me!' I tread a few more steps. 'Excuse me!' Everyone is ignoring me! After a long walk I reach the door. On opening it I see a bed, I am lying in it attached to a heart monitor. I am confused. I can only hear one continuous sound: *...beep...*

ALEXANDER GRANT (12)
Silcoates School, Wakefield

The Ghost At 12 O'Clock

The clock struck twelve. My spine shivered, my skin was cold while my heart was beating out of my chest. I edged on and I saw something move in the distance, it was a silhouette of something. The place was eerie, but I still had the courage to keep going on upstairs. As I turned round I saw the most peculiar thing, it was a ghost. After I could blink I was impaled as I screamed to my death 'Argh!'

Olivia Lee (11)
Silcoates School, Wakefield

Alone

As I entered the dark and gloomy moor, I had a cold slug of fear which shivered down my spine. As I trudged my way through the sinister looking moor, it felt like somebody had stabbed me with an icy cold dagger! Suddenly I heard... a crash, and a shriek. My heart pounded like a drum as I peered into the darkness like a golden eagle! In this lonely darkness I spotted a girl... with eyes as red as blood and a body as dead as a dodo edging towards me. One million words hit me but one was clear... Run!

Ben John Chafer (11)
Silcoates School, Wakefield

The Return Of Slasher

The dark sky fell onto the discreet cabin. I was doing some drawings. My favourite was one with dark eyes and a hockey mask. He had a bullet-proof jacket under a ripped raincoat. Slasher! I saw a tree outside that said, 'I'm coming'. My heart pounded like a bass drum. Then the door opened. A man with a hockey mask came in. He had a ripped rain jacket, tight boots and was holding a razor-sharp machete. He came towards me. He raised his arm looking at me.
'Stop,' I said. 'Please don't.'
He stopped. 'Die!'

Kurt Johnson (11)
Silcoates School, Wakefield

Watched

It was a foggy night, you couldn't see anything. Jack and his best friend Will were tramping through the forest. They ignored the sign not knowing what they were up against... Jack said he felt like he was being watched. Will agreed. But what they were being watched by was not a normal kid that thinks he's hard but something very deadly! They kept on walking then saw this yellow dot. They didn't realise that they'd turned red. Then they knew what they were. They were eyes. Will fell down to the earthy ground...

Ben George Yule (11)
Silcoates School, Wakefield

Horror Graveyard

We just needed to go through the village of decaying gravestones. We were all petrified. We all banded together and our teeth were chattering in horror. We opened the gate a tiny bit and it sounded like scraping your nails down a blackboard. We took a small step, it was pitch-black. It made our eyes fill up with tears. The street lights were flickering on and off. We took another step, we saw a shadow run across us. We looked round, I saw two big beady eyes looking down at us. We saw another shadow. Dan felt a breath on his neck.

Dan Jack Yule (11)
Silcoates School, Wakefield

The Reflected Truth

I reached the end of the corridor. The door was locked. There was no escape. I heard the whispers heading my way. I smelt dried blood that was worse than the faint whistling wind that travelled down the corridor, through one ear and echoing, chanting noises out the other. It came closer. My tongue felt like burnt pizza crust.
'It was you,' the voice called.
The constant tension made me sweat and shake as my hairs stood up straight on my skin. It came out of the shadows, holding a mirror. Reflecting that I was the true monster after all.

Henri Poole-Birrell (14)
Stover School, Newton Abbot

Silenced

A blood-curdling scream echoed ominously across the village. All too quickly I found myself and the whole village in front of the mangled and dismembered body of a young girl, Abigail. Rumours spread like wildfire, talk of the Devil and witchcraft. Only Abigail and I knew the truth, but of course the dead do not tell secrets. As the sun went down the mayor ordered us to go home and lock our doors.
That night as I lay in bed consumed by darkness, I knew I was next and there was nothing I could do but wait...

Lara-Louise Jones (14)
Stover School, Newton Abbot

Pleading With The Walls

On his knees with an expression of utmost despair, Alexander pleaded with the wall. 'I didn't mean to hurt her,' he protested profusely even though no one was listening. 'She was my special girl. She was my Polly. I loved her.' But love is obsessive and consuming. A glint of fire gleamed in his eyes and for a moment he seemed equal to the devil. In a coarse voice he growled, 'I warned her but she didn't listen. She should have listened.'
Only a day previously they had found Polly: torn open, empty sockets, hacked flesh. They hadn't found her lover.

Rose Smith (15)
Stover School, Newton Abbot

Matches

The sack over his head told George he was in trouble. The distinctive aroma of tar reinforced those fears. It wisped up his nose like a disease, making him cough and splutter from the strength of the smell. George heard a match being flicked and then blown out. 'You were the one with the matches, weren't you? After the harvest? You held my hand over the flame and watched me scream.' The floorboards creaked underfoot as the old church strained against the wind and thunder. 'Have you ever wondered what it's like to burn, George?' A match flicked on again.

Ben Hooper (14)
Stover School, Newton Abbot

What Dwells Beneath

The sun had set and an eerie and sombre mist fell upon the entrance to the catacombs. The ancient tunnels reminded me of a nightmarish underworld which I dreaded entering alone, not knowing what sinister things awaited me. Mysterious inscriptions enlivened the walls, luring me in further than I ever should have dared to venture. Gradually the walls drew tighter as if they urged me to turn back while I still could, before I became lost in the macabre labyrinth. Amid a haunting chill I sensed that in these lonely catacombs, I was not alone. Devilish eyes fixed upon mine...

Amy Adams (17)
Stover School, Newton Abbot

Your Fears Will Be Gone

The darkness was thick like melting wax, heavily sliding from above. It made breathing hard, squeezing Judith's chest. This feeling reminded her about silly old fairy tales about monsters like vampires, but these stories didn't look funny anymore, chilling her spine and making her body tremble with terror. 'Mommy,' she called quietly, 'I'm scared!'
Thin fingers touched her shoulder as a sparkle of hope. 'Do not worry sweetheart. I'll kiss you and your fears will be gone.' A slight touch of cold lips on the girl's neck. Claws. Warm blood. She was not afraid anymore.

Irina Chernousova (17)
Stover School, Newton Abbot

A Cold Hug

I woke to the sound of my wife calling me down for breakfast. I lay in bed for a couple more minutes listening to her wonderful tunes while she was boiling the eggs. She was humming to the tune of 'London's Burning'. Suddenly, out of the corner of my eye, I noticed a bright light. I sat up and there was a blazing fire at the end of my bed. I called for my wife. I froze, my eyes widened as I felt that there was a slight rustle in the duvet and a cold arm wrapped around me.

Felix De Ganay (12)
The Harrodian School, London

The Reflection

My hand reaches towards the matte, brass handle. The door momentarily shudders before giving in and jarring open. I enter. Just a while ago I could've sworn I heard a noise coming from up here, yet nothing seems disturbed. Still convinced I am not mad, I venture on. To my right appears a mirror. So, as any woman would, I look at it. A horrific shriek leaves my lips, for behind me quivers a ghostly apparition. I turn around. Nothing. Again, in the mirror it's there. I turn around... nothing. Suddenly an icy, cold hand lies on my shoulder. It's there.

Iona Oliver (11)
The Harrodian School, London

Hush Little Baby

One cold night there lived a young woman called Margaret who was making her tea before she went to watch her favourite TV programme, when suddenly upstairs she heard her one-year-old baby jumping around and screaming. Without hesitation she walked up the endless spiralling staircase until she got to the top of the stairs. She turned right, the baby's room was now in sight but for some reason she couldn't hear the baby anymore and there was a cold chill in the air. As Margaret opened the door to the room she saw that it was tucked up perfectly.

Frederick Hales (11)
The Harrodian School, London

SMOKE

We were making hot chocolate and ascending the staircase in her house. It was freezing outside, wind sweeping over the trees. I was delighted to be cosy in her old house. As we were walking, I stuck up my nose and was about to point out that a stench of thick smoke was spreading around her home. I opened my mouth, but she noticed, and immediately said, 'Do you smell smoke?'
I replied, 'What is it?'
The response was creepy. 'I remember a couple of years ago an old man died, he was known for his love of cigars...'

SOPHIE MUIJSER (11)
The Harrodian School, London

THE SHADOW

I was home alone and my parents told me not to open the door to anybody. It was about 9pm and there was a knock on the door. I walked over cautiously to the security camera and saw a shadow and I started panicking. I called my dad on my mobile phone. My dad told me to ignore it. I looked outside from my window and the shadow wasn't there. I went downstairs to investigate. I opened the front door and there was nothing there. I turned around and there was the shadow standing still, nothing causing it to move.

ARSENY OSIPOV (12)
The Harrodian School, London

She Followed

'Don't go in... Don't go in!' She followed even though she didn't want to. The door flung open, we looked around suspiciously. I crept in. She followed. The windows were covered with a thick layer of mould and dust, only a gloomy light could filter in. We scurried through the eerie corridor. The ground was peppered with the bodies of dead flies, lying motionless. I covered my nose to keep out the putrefying smell of death. I loomed into a musty room. She followed. All the corners were secretive places, no one had explored. I turned away. She didn't follow...

Nara-May Rishani (11)
The Harrodian School, London

Don't Miss Her

I turned around and she prowled into someone's front garden. I ran back down the road to get there before she caused any damage. I got to the gate of the garden, I looked round. When I focused my eyes on the floor in the garden I looked around and she wasn't there. The garden hadn't been damaged. I looked all over the garden, there was no way for her to escape. Not over the wall, nowhere. Suddenly I heard a bark from behind me. I turned around and there she was, sitting on the ground panting with her tongue.

Daisy Kingston (11)
The Harrodian School, London

He Was Gone

The grandfather clock struck nine. It was time to go. I pushed the door open, just to check it was locked. It fell open whilst a gust of wind brushed my face and ran into the restaurant. I went upstairs where my bag was. There was an eerie silence. I looked outside, only to find that a thick fog had rolled in. I walked downstairs whilst someone went upstairs. It was an old man, who was heading for the staff room. I felt suspicious. I got downstairs and realised that my keys were upstairs. The old man was not there anymore!

Phoenix Barnett (11)
The Harrodian School, London

The Cold Chill

It was a dark, stormy winter's night and Katy was coming home from work. When she got back to her flat she saw that her window was open. That was strange. She was sure she had closed it before she left. Katy shut her window. When she came back after dinner her front door was open. She was sure this time she had closed it behind her. Suddenly she heard a strange sound. 'Hello, is anyone there?' Then Katy felt the cold chill of a nasty presence in the very room. Then she felt it again. She turned around and saw a...

William Baker (11)
The Harrodian School, London

What Earthquake?

12:00pm, January 19th 1998. A cold stormy night. The thundering rain pounded on the candlelit street with the silence of an abandoned house. Suddenly, the lights flickered off and on, forcing me to lock the emerald green door. Ottso witnessed his diamond chandelier collapse as the wind blew stronger, causing the floor to shake. He decided to call the police since a piece of glass fell on his knee. Sue, the police officer, whispered with fear, 'There is no earthquake that has taken place at your address.'
Ottso was thinking, *what just happened and who is doing this to me?*

Isabel Beiboer (11)
The Harrodian School, London

The Ghost Painting!

I was puzzled. I was sure, in fact convinced, that before, the painting I was staring at - the one in the antique frame covered in cobwebs - had a distinct image of an elderly lady. Frowning, I squeezed my eyes and studied it again. This time she'd faded up to the hips. Her legs were missing. I shook my head, *Am I dreaming? This can't be right...?* By the third glance she was gone, completely gone. I glared at the hail shooting down from the sky like bullets. Then I noticed the elderly lady in the mirror quickly pass by!

Georgia Cowell (11)
The Harrodian School, London

Last Night?

I was running from the horror I'd just seen.
I could still hear her voice cackling behind me... 'You cannot escape me, boy!'
Seeing my house, I sighed shakily. Opening the door, I stepped inside and smiled.
Suddenly, I heard water running upstairs. I climbed upstairs to investigate! I felt a cold breath behind me. Cowering in fear, I turned around slowly and froze before the scene in front of me! There she was, standing tall and proud in all her glamour.
Then I heard it again... 'You cannot escape me, boy!'
I turned and fled down the creaking stairs.

Isabelle Primicerio (11)
The Harrodian School, London

Scratched

Swiftly I yank down the yellowing sheets of the furniture. A swarm of dust flies up and I start to cough. Alone. Quiet. Dread. I pull down another few sheets and I find a floor-length mirror. The edge is etched with leaves; rust has started to loom its way onto the mirror. I pull down a few more sheets, an old portrait of the family glares down at me. Suddenly a screech hits my ears and I fall backwards onto a table. As I get up I glance up at the painting. The eyes are scribbled out. Haunted. Scratched.

Millie Fooks (12)
The Harrodian School, London

Bricks

The golden sun blazed through my window. I was sitting by the chimney waiting for my sister to come. When I heard the ancient chimney whistling like a kettle, I opened the door to the chimney, there was nothing there and the whistling had stopped. I sat back thinking to myself, *that's strange.* Suddenly the whistling started again but louder and more powerful. As I reached out for the door I saw it, a shadow twice as big as me getting bigger and bigger as it got closer and closer. I turned around, nothing - and then I felt the hand.

Claudia Bo Beaumont (11)
The Harrodian School, London

Lost For Words

Bang! The door slammed behind me. Angry tears trickled down my blood-flushed cheeks. I ran towards the gloomy forest, fog wove around the towering ominous trees. It behaved like a spiteful splenetic snake, strangling its prey. A vigorous chain of hurtful words flowed from my mouth while the dark, sinister clouds came creeping in. I found myself deep in mysterious undergrowth, my head filled with dismay. I panicked, what should I do? I fell to the ground, sobbing. Suddenly, rain started malevolently pouring down on me. A piercing, blood-curdling scream froze me, taking all my bravery away.

Ines Verhoosel (11)
The Harrodian School, London

The Orchestra

I'm sleeping in my new bed. It's midnight and the only sound is rain pattering against my window. Suddenly I hear the door creaking open and closed and the cupboard door is slamming open and shut and the black phone is ringing deafeningly. This orchestra of noises is rising in volume, one new item making a noise at a time. I am relieved to see my mum at our doorstep outside the window. The tension is rising as she scrambles for her keys. But, wait! A black shadow is creeping up and... it's just swept her up into thin air!

Leya Himani (11)
The Harrodian School, London

Frost Bite

As I strode through the forest, the fresh smell of pine crept up my nostrils. Icicles clung from the arms of the huge trees that towered over me. As I gently placed my delicate finger on one of the icicles, a sharp coldness pierced my skin, sending a shiver down my spine. *Shudder!* It was getting unbearably cold! My hands felt like they were being stabbed a million times. I hid them under my gloves. I was making my way home when... suddenly, everything went silent, intense and ominous. A cold, icy hand clutched my shoulder. I froze, terror-stricken.

Anna Tatham (11)
The Harrodian School, London

A Cold Touch

I walked out of the office alone into the empty, deserted street. The moon shone brightly in the cloudy sky as I made my way home. A shiver was sent down my spine as I wandered, feeling like I was being followed. I reached the flats and fumbled for my keys, worrying that someone was about to jump out at me. I went through the door and was comforted by the sound of it closing behind me. Then, as my arm reached for the banister, I felt a cold, shaking finger touch my tingling hand.

Isabela Pond (11)
The Harrodian School, London

Lost

Swirls of grey mist gnarled their fingers around the roots of looming oak trees exuding an aura of mystery and suspense. The forest, once teeming with life, was now desolate and deathly silence cloaked the ghostly region. All I could hear was the sound of my own ragged breath as I stumbled like a blind person through the inky blackness. A blood-curdling scream shattered the silence like glass and made me catch my breath. Suddenly I knew that I was not alone. My heart started pounding against my ribcage as I realised that I was not going home.

Iris Annabel Goldsmith (11)
The Harrodian School, London

A Christmas Fright

It was a dreary Christmas Eve when nobody dared step outside. There was one man, a Christmas hater, and every year something came around to haunt him just like he did to children.
There was a dark presence in the room. I noticed the front door was slightly open. I thought I had shut it; clearly not. I put on my dressing gown and lay on my bed. As I was reading I heard a creak in the door. I rushed under my bed and waited, waited. A figure soared through my room and I knew this was my last Christmas...

Tristan Anderson
The Harrodian School, London

The Presence

Gulping nervously, Rosie took a small step inside the abandoned, dark hallway. Fog crept into the cracked, broken window next to the glowing candle that hovered like a luminous ghost. Cackling voices entered Rosie's head whilst she tiptoed up the huge winding stairs like a frightened mouse. Wispy cobwebs were draped across the handrail as if they were clinging on for dear life. Suddenly, a colossal wooden door creaked open like a screeching child. A cold, numbing breath possessed Rosie's shivering neck killing any signs of innocence. Ghostly hands wrapped secretly around Rosie's waist, warning her that she wasn't alone.

Jude Araim (12)
The Harrodian School, London

The Gothic House

The desolate house stood all alone. It had been abandoned many, many years ago. With gutters hanging loosely, it looked derelict and neglected. It was a ghostly looking house with gargoyles perched on each side of the roof. They appeared to be screaming at me, warning me to stay away. They were there to protect this house. The windowpanes were broken and jagged. Green ivy climbed all over the face of the house, wrapping itself around the drainpipes, like a snake trying to suffocate its prey. The large oak door stood open like a huge mouth, beckoning me in...

Jackson Grout (11)
The Harrodian School, London

The Murder Mansion

Midnight. Fog cakes the room with an eerie, grey blanket. Lightning flashes around me, scarring the sky. I The misty moon stares down at me. I hear a scream from a young girl in the distance. I take one glance back but nothing is there. I sprint to the nearest house as my body breaks into a cold sweat. I take one glimpse back and a young girl in a nightdress is there with a broken china doll. I run into the old, worn-out house. Slowly, I sit down in an old chair. I'm petrified. I feel a cold presence - she's there...

Alexandra Kuaale Torpe (11)
The Harrodian School, London

The Rustle In The Bush

The murky fog had already swiftly crept in, and the deserted house bathed in it. I ignored that the emerald ivy crawled around the mysterious house and that the thundering roar of the wind deafened me. I came here for one reason only, and it was to find Ellie. 'Ellie!' I bellowed over the wailing wind. There was no response from Ellie, but there was a weak rustle in the bush followed by a menacing snare. I knew I wasn't alone. I knew I would encounter whatever stole Ellie.

Luna Banon (12)
The Harrodian School, London

Follow The Black Bird

Trembling, my two left feet thumping against the cold ground is the only thing to be heard. Reluctantly I carry on following the crow. Its dark yellow eyes pierced mine. Paranoid the crow will haunt me for the rest of my life. A cold rush of wind strangled me. The crow lifted its delicate wings and hovered inside a dilapidated snug home. My heart was throbbing harder than ever. As I stepped inside, the door whined in pain. 'Hello!' I screamed. All I heard was twinkling of a lullaby. I almost felt like... like... like sleeping...
'Hush!' cackled a voice.

Arnella Rapoport (11)
The Harrodian School, London

World's End

It was a cold, moonlit night when I drove down the bumpy gravel path towards the manor house. I felt suddenly that I was being watched. Then I came in sight of the menacing gargoyles on top of the old creepy manor which had been broken, battered and beaten by the torrential rain. I got out of the car and the cold air penetrated my skin. I walked into the house past the colossal black door and moved upstairs. Suddenly the air became colder, and there was a shadowy presence. Then the phone rang. Then, the screaming began...

Lucas Brownson (11)
The Harrodian School, London

The Cabin In The Woods

The luminous moon was like a tear in a black cloth. I could see it clearly through the broken window of the cabin I was hiding in. Night had come quickly and I was nowhere near home, deep in the woods, terrified. Something was outside, something not human, scratching at the flimsy door. I flung myself at the window as the door crashed open. I could smell its rotten breath. I leapt out and ran... but the trees deceived me and I smashed into one and fell. The last thing I saw were two enormous red eyes.

Gabriel Langan (11)
The Harrodian School, London

THE HAUNTED HOSPITAL

It was a quiet and gloomy night; no one to be heard along the lonely street except a few murmurs every now and then. In the distance, there was a building with no lights on. However there was a faint figure lurking around. A head looked through the window. Alfred, who was 93, saw a shadow creeping around. He fell asleep with shock. One night, he couldn't handle it and went to investigate. He heard a cry and a gasp. All of a sudden, it stopped. A cold hand tapped his shoulder. Alfred darted around. He saw his long-lost wife.

KIARA WILSON (11)
The Harrodian School, London

THE WRONG HOUSE

As I approached the sullen, torn down village, my heart sank six feet. I gaped in dismay at what was meant to be a holiday. The deepest darkest stars stabbed the cold November night with a dull poorly lit haze. As I turned the key, the candlelit oak door was beckoning me in with my every breath. The water quivered in ripples as the moon shone boldly with pride. The half-open windows were dancing in the wind, they were suspended by only a single rusting hinge. I entered. My heart stopped. The wind wailed, the door slammed shut. I screamed!

CONOR WILLIAMS (11)
The Harrodian School, London

The Chilling Encounter

Swirling fog surrounded the shadowy graveyard, making it hard to see anyone or anything. An eerie silence filled the air. A crescent moon, high in the sky, peered down inquisitively at me. My family had disappeared into the frightening gloom. I was alone. My heart started to pound. My hands started to tremble. 'Mum? Dad? Are you there?' I called. No reply. 'Hello? Anyone?' The whispering wind whipped into an ice gale, charging through everything in its path. It felt as if there was a wicked force controlling the wind; it appeared to be following me, pushing me, taunting me.

Sophia Bicknell (11)
The Harrodian School, London

The Wolves Of Terror

Silence. The door handle turned. The door yawned open. I stepped in. Shadows slunk around the huge magenta curtains, blocking the little light there was. I lit a candle like a solitary figure standing against an army of darkness. The rain pounded against the roof, soaking through. A musty smell hit me. Then suddenly a sporadic tapping reverberated through the house. The little wolves of terror crept closer. I checked behind the curtain but nothing was there. I looked through the window, the only thing to meet my eyes was hundreds of miles of bleak mountains. Then a floorboard creaked...

Kiyo Brandreth-Stroud (11)
The Harrodian School, London

It Is Time

There was no looking back, I knew it was here. Silently, I increased my pace without saying a word. The moon was like a sun shimmering over the hundreds of dead bodies. Every gravestone looked the same: grey, dusty and wearing away. As I was running I heard a laugh coming from behind. It was time and I knew it. Thunder was crashing, lightning was exploding and rain was pouring. The figure from behind was getting closer and closer until - *bang!* Everything stopped. No thunder, no lightning and no rain! I was starting to slow down, beginning to walk but then it was too late.

Calypso Simonian (11)
The Harrodian School, London

The Suspicious House Next To The Loch

Mist was crawling in, through the house, to the kitchen. An eerie silence surrounded me as the crisp, autumn leaves flooded onto the rosewood floor. Darkness swirled around me like a blanket being wrapped around my body. Slowly walking, a rusty door latch lay before my eyes. I tried to twist it but it wouldn't budge. Finally after a few minutes, door creaked open and it led downstairs into a murky basement. Taking a few steps down to the unknown, the hazy basement welcomed me but suddenly the door locked behind me. I knew I was not alone.

Amber Jackson (11)
The Harrodian School, London

Darkness

The darkness was all around me. I stood there shivering in the cold, moonlit air. The smell of rotting corpses filled my nostrils as I waited in the graveyard. Then I heard a noise, I looked back, nothing was there but I felt like someone was watching me. I ran. As I was running I saw a big mansion with a huge door - the handle was old and rusty. I turned it. Inside it was dark and gloomy, one of the windows was broken and the wind was gushing through the window. The window was rusty and dusty.

Imogen Katherine Sophia Barbour (12)
The Harrodian School, London

The Sinister

'Don't worry, it shouldn't be too bad,' I reassured myself as I walked along the nice, but peculiar, corridor. I turned around the corner to find a mysterious-looking door. I walked towards the door, candelabra in hand, and turned the rosewood handle. The door made an eerie creak and opened. The first thing I saw was a beautiful painting of a beautiful woman. There was something underneath it which I could not make out. I walked further into the strange room and saw an ominous shattered mirror. 'Hee-hee!' I heard a demonic laugh and the door locking. I froze.

Ayaan Ansari (11)
The Harrodian School, London

The Hooded Figure

The gate banged shut behind her. An owl hooted, breaking the silence. She was inside now. Her breathing was rapidly quickening. Her skin was as pale as snow. It wasn't a chilly night, however, as soon as she was in the unkempt garden, she started to shiver. She could feel someone watching her. She spun around and a hooded figure stood motionless, watching her. Her heart beat so fast against her chest it was almost as if it wasn't even beating. She sprinted inside the forbidding house. The first room she ran into had mirrors everywhere. Behind her was the figure.

Isara Burgess (11)
The Harrodian School, London

The Church On The Hill

It was cold, my toes felt like they were solid ice. The freezing mud of the wet marsh covered my ragged bare feet. All I could think of was reaching my destination, the church on the hill. Each painful stagger I took made me feel like my consciousness was leaving me. It felt like I was getting further away from the church with every lurch I made. The little amount of dingy moonlight that shone upon my path disappeared. I could see nothing. I collapsed, making my whole body drenched in the soggy mud. All hope that I had, gone.

Otto Hall (12)
The Harrodian School, London

Trapped!

The sleeping grey clouds encroached on the luminous moon. The inky-black darkness was swallowing me up. The trees were grabbing me. The roaring, screeching wind, louder than a thousand screaming girls was earsplitting. I had reached the gnarled and ancient door of a gloomy Victorian house. I knocked on the door hoping for shelter for the cold was biting at my skin and the rain was spitting down on me. There was no answer. Desperate for warmth, I pushed the door open and stepped inside the house. As I was creeping along the antiquated corridor the door slammed shut.

Agnes Chappell (11)
The Harrodian School, London

The Woods

The clouds were towering over me as I walked deeper into the woods. The trees rustled in the distance. As the woods called me in, I shuddered. As I entered the wood it was like they were grabbing me. Branches loomed over me. Something snapped, I jumped straight out of my skin. Was it me or was there someone else in here? The fog waved at me in the distance it was so sinister, threatening. Looking around me through the gloom I saw something approaching me. What was it? A figure dressed in black and white came up to me and said, 'Run!'

Emily Tremayne (11)
The Harrodian School, London

The Icy Breath

As James crept down the desolate alleyway, he sensed an ominous presence. The street lights were flickering violently. James felt a breath so cold it was like an iceberg smashed into his neck. He turned round sharply to find that he was all alone. James was left perplexed by the freezing breath. Self-consciously he realised that he was jogging. As James started to pace himself he peered through apprehensive eyes and noticed that there were two shadows. His mind raced as he found himself paralysed by terror. An icy chill consumed him. Then he heard, 'You are not alone.'

Donovan Morrison (11)
The Harrodian School, London

The Grip

The sky looked like bad, mouldy milk. My throat was dry and sore. The temptation to run away was high. But I didn't. The woods held me captive. Wonder chilled my veins. The trees made me feel enchanted. The frosty branches that looked like bony, decrepit fingers embraced me tightly. I wasn't agitated, just clueless. I stared down at my pale legs. Mother never lets me out by myself. Never. Suddenly, the foliage held me tauter. My bones dug into my stomach. Bile burned at the back of my mouth. I was frozen, frozen in time.

Lily Van Der Gag (11)
The Harrodian School, London

Nothing...

It was a pitch-black night. The dark clouds were kidnapping the shining moon. I wasn't going to get back to the hotel in time. I started rushing as I could hear the wind howling like a werewolf. The doors were chunky and made out of a dark brown type of wood; the cracks looked like they were going to fall over like a giant pushing it. As aghast as a person in a pitch-black room, I walked in. The old woman invited me in. I got straight into bed. I felt a cold hand stroking my head. Nothing...

Pietro Hill (11)
The Harrodian School, London

A Dark Surprise

The lonely, decaying walls of the forgotten alleyway glared down at the cold, weeping girl. She wore a deep red petticoat that almost screamed against the gloomy atmosphere. She ran hastily towards the comforting glow from the windows of the library. The golden doorknob was a frosty winter's morning against her shaking hand. As she entered the room, the warmth curled its soft yet ominous fingers around her. The floorboards creaked with every step she took, and all of a sudden the lights flickered out. At that same moment all the comfort in her blew out like a single flame.

Emma Warren (11)
The Harrodian School, London

RED NOSE

It was a dark, misty night and my parents were going out. My mum told me to call the old lady next door if anything was wrong. After about ten minutes I looked out the window. A clown stood a hundred metres away with a knife and a baton. I rushed to the telephone and called the lady next door. 'There is nothing there,' she said in confusion. I went back to the TV, there it was again! I rang again. 'There is nothing there, I'll be over in ten!' she insisted.
I looked, a red nose lay motionless on the gravel...

FLYNN WILLIAM SWINSCOE (11)
The Harrodian School, London

TIME IS RUNNING OUT

The fog twirled in front of me, making me feel nauseous as the opaque, gloomy, stone path bounced ahead. Suddenly a huge pair of ancient gates appeared out of thin air. There was an intimidating feeling. Next to the gates there were two gargoyles on the pillars. The gates had an extremely big padlock resting on the concrete. The gargoyles on the columns had cracks all over them. But looking closer, the cracks were the same. The eyes of the gargoyles started to glow a sombre red. 'The time has come, child,' whispered the gargoyles softly. 'The time has come.'

MATILDA PAGE (11)
The Harrodian School, London

Church?

Wandering aimlessly around the frigid, cobbled, misty streets after dark was an unnerving place. All of the rundown ancient shopfronts were even more unattractive after nightfall.
The streets bore the remnants of tourists during the day. The fantastic spine-chilling architecture of the cathedral stood out from the sprawling suburbs. However, the magnificent church had never been used for unknown reasons. If you asked anyone what happened they would pretend that they hadn't heard.
The church was soon to be knocked down but as the bulldozer began its final approach a chorus of singing was heard.

Louis Christopher Hodge (11)
The Harrodian School, London

Not Alone

Reluctantly, I continued walking towards the heart of the forest. The damp, dewy leaves glistened in the illuminated night sky. The bright, full moon was wrapped up in clouds like a newborn baby. I continued making my way towards the veiled danger. With every step I could feel the crisp, dry ground crunch underneath my feet. After a few moments the trees became more and more menacing and the darkness had started dispelling all light. Sinister and reckless shadows seemed to creep out of the undergrowth and cling to the bushes. Hearing someone pursuing me, I spun...

Theresia Schwab (12)
The Harrodian School, London

The Alleyway

Gazing up at the harvest moon through a silhouette of roofs, I hurried down the dark alleyway. The tapping of my shoes was not the only sound I could hear: a quiet scraping sound followed my footsteps. Hastily, I quickened my pace. A pair of colourless eyes glared into mine and a cold shudder went down my back. The ashen-faced man whispered hoarsely, 'Good evening Madam.'

I suddenly, inexplicably, felt the urge that the figure in front of me was a hissing snake. He reached out his hand to grasp mine. As I took it unwillingly, I involuntarily shuddered.

Nerys Williams (12)
The Harrodian School, London

Lost And Lonely

The trees started to rustle violently. As I looked around to close the window, suddenly the trees stopped. I walked downstairs and heard the slam of my bedroom door, which was odd as I hadn't left it open. Feeling lost and lonely, I was sure I caught a glimpse of a figure outside. As the lights had never worked, I picked up my glowing candle and had a look outside to see if that dark figure was maybe lost. I decided to head inside and as I was doing so, lights unexpectedly flashed on and off.

Mia Cain (11)
The Harrodian School, London

The Retired Music Shop

Midnight struck. The retired music shop towered over me. Whispers were beckoning me in. I turned around, the morose street was empty. I turned back and opened the door. I entered the room. A creak came from behind me but nothing was there. I took a step forward and the door shut behind me. I turned round to turn the light on and the piano started to play. It got faster and faster. I felt a chill run down my back. I felt a breath on my neck...

Olivia Kentish (11)
The Harrodian School, London

The Town

There it was, the old town that no one had set foot in for thirty years. A large pub stood in the middle of the town, still slowly crumbling. The door, which was unwilling to open, finally opened, revealing the mess inside. Beer glasses were smashed on the ground, everything had been thrown around. I decided to get a drink from one of the old beer pumps, even though it would taste rank. I grabbed a glass and pulled the tap. It squeaked and the yellow liquid filled the cup. That's when I noticed the black figure staring at me.

Finnian Hess (11)
The Harrodian School, London

The Cigar

It was time to discuss my father's will. Silently, a tear crept from my eye. His absence was an anchor sinking a ship: me. Clutching on to his silver cigar case, I could almost feel his presence through the reassuring object, a spiritual flow pulsing through my veins. Abruptly, there was a knock on the door, it had an unusual rhythm and sounded almost melancholy. I answered. No one was there but I smelt a familiar musk which I would know anywhere. I looked to the source; a great, gracious, glowing, solitary star in a lonely night sky: a cigar.

Freddie Bowyer (11)
The Harrodian School, London

Do You Believe Now?

'Of course I don't believe!' I said, with a stupid grin on my face.
'You sure?' she asked, with a grin that was stupider than mine. 'Okay, listen to this: two girls were having a sleepover,' she said.
'Like this one?' I asked in fear.
She shot an evil look and nodded. 'Yes but one of the girls had a deep secret. The clock struck twelve, and her soul flipped over, so she stabbed her friend.' She was interrupted by the clock which struck twelve. 'Perfect timing,' she said.
I was confused, well, until she pulled out a knife from behind her.

Maddi O'Meara (11)
The Harrodian School, London

The Shadow Of A Woman

I looked at my digital clock, it was 6.00am. Suddenly, a shadow of a tall woman came towards me slowly, carrying a sharp curved dagger about 21cm long. I was petrified and pale. I couldn't move. The shadow kept getting closer and closer. Then she crept up at me with her long nails and grabbed my head, with a firm grip and sliced my head right off. Phew! I woke up, it was just a bad dream. It was 5.59am, the numbers in bright red. Then the clock struck 6.00am. The old closet door, made out of rosewood, creaked open...

Raquel Alonso Zurutuza (12)
The Harrodian School, London

Alone

The night air thickened around me, searching everything around this lonely, deserted street. Usually the pale fog would disappear with a thundering hiss that would bounce from each jagged wall to the next one, but today was different. It never went, it just painfully stood there, alone and helpless in the illuminated streetlights. 'Hello.' My word only plunged back at me, like a scared child running away from the monster under their bed. The damp air entered my lungs like smoke filling a room. I couldn't breathe. My body stiffened and I froze to the spot, paralysed with fear.

Paige Chamberlain (11)
The Harrodian School, London

The Visitor

The moon glared at me as if calling my name, hissing at me to go in. Fearfully I got closer until finally I was at the door, hands trembling, sweat dripping from my face and hands. Slowly I stepped into the mansion. All the walls were dull, paint peeling off. The floors damp, they creaked everywhere I stepped. Every room was poorly lit. A small crack in the window let a slither of moonlight through. The wind became stronger and roared as it hit the window. Suddenly I heard an earsplitting smash. The room became colder and the lights turned out.

Tatiana Fein-Hughes (11)
The Harrodian School, London

Fear Of The Unknown

As I looked around I heard a few distant creaks and noises on the floor above. I looked around at the furniture and saw that it was a mahogany-brown table and chair. The eerie door slowly screeched open and revealed the room which looked murky. As I went up the stairs swiftly, I looked around just to see if anything was present with me. Staggering across the dim and murky hallway I heard a faint moan. Swiftly I went into that room with fear, stepped back, knew it was only a rat that ran past. I ran out immediately.

Kamran Behbehani (12)
The Harrodian School, London

What Happens After Midnight?

Midnight. Darkness surrounded me, blinding me. Silence swooped in, the air was stale. Musty smells filled my lungs. What was that? Nothing. I caught the scent of burning and cautiously looked around but the darkness had left my eyes hollow. A candle was sitting in the middle of the hallway, twisting and turning like a snake-charmer beckoning its victim. Suddenly I heard a noise, a long painful groan. When I looked back the candle was gone. I staggered around the pitch-black room feeling for a door. I found one and slammed it behind me. Finally, I opened my eyes and I realised something was wrong. This room doesn't exist.

Grace Donavan-Lafuente (11)
The Harrodian School, London

The Deserted Forest

Midnight. The sky was inky black. There was a sudden howl from a wolf on a jagged rock. In front of me there was an abandoned mansion, it was surrounded by fog and was being shadowed by the moon. I went inside and suddenly the door shut. I walked into the kitchen and I saw an axe with blood dripping from it. At that moment I heard footsteps approaching. I had been followed. Immediately I ran out of the kitchen then the door opened as if telling me to leave. I ran out and never went back.

Kian Soroush (11)
The Harrodian School, London

Untitled

Fog and mist blanketed the dark graveyard. I could smell death all around. As I went to a nearby old crooked hut there was a hanging portrait of a shadowy person with one eye and when I moved anywhere it followed me. I was too horrified. I ran back to the foggy graveyard. Then a small flicker of moonlight came down and I saw a distant shadow. Suddenly a large branch broke off the tree behind me. I was shocked,. Then a faint scream was heard in my ear. I was isolated, nowhere to run or hide.

Dean Khan Dhillon (11)
The Harrodian School, London

Midnight Forest

The wind howled and whistled as it meandered through the trees. The tall trees stood erect as the deadly moonlight cut through the branches. A blanket of darkness had engulfed the land, forcing it to be night. My heart raced for I was last in this gloomy forest. Would I ever get out? The leaves crunched beneath my sodden boots. Behind me, a twig snapped. I swung round but there was nothing there. A colossal clap of thunder bellowed across the earth as the rain poured down my cheeks. Suddenly, I heard a whispering voice calling out the word death...

Charlotte Georgia Van Lomwel (12)
The Harrodian School, London

Dreaming?

The damned creature flailed over me, clawing at my flesh, tearing wildly at my skin. Oozing red blood had soaked its way through and splattered almost everything in the room. The immense pain overwhelmed me. I slipped in and out of consciousness. The last thing I laid my eyes on was the clock flashing 22:07 before the darkness swallowed me and I blacked out.
I awoke, thank goodness, it was all just a dream. I glanced towards my bedside table, the digital clock blinked 22:06 and I slowly turned my head as I heard the wardrobe door slowly creak open...

Amy Swash (14)
Tettenhall College, Wolverhampton

Daddy Is That You?

My best friend Millie has moved away. When I ask Mom where she has gone she just ignores me. Millie didn't tell me she was going away, I wonder why? Millie and I tell each other everything, so this officially makes us not best friends anymore. Every night at eight o'clock Daddy comes into my room, kisses my head and says, 'See you in the morning, Princess.' Last night Daddy didn't come in at eight so I just went to sleep, but then I heard a voice that wasn't my daddy's saying, 'Come and play with all the other children.'

McKenna Joni-Mae Maddox (15)
Tettenhall College, Wolverhampton

Killer Identity

Splutter, splat! My car breaks down. I'm stranded in the middle of nowhere! I switch on the radio for comfort, only to hear that a serial killer is on the loose. The wind howls outside and rain beats against the car window. I turn my head to the sound of empty footsteps outside but nobody is there. Suddenly, a figure appears outside my car and to my delight it's a policeman. He escorts me to his car for safety. I clamber into the car to find a dead body stuffed in the back seat. Trapped!

Suvraj Pejatta (12)
Tettenhall College, Wolverhampton

Who Moved The Glass?

The four members' fingers were pressed against the glass. At that moment, the glass jumped from letter to letter, rapidly pulling them towards each letter - spelling out Joshua. Suddenly, all three other members ran out of the room, screeching and dragging each other out of the darkly-lit basement.
Only then did one girl humorously exclaim, 'Okay who pushed it?'
'Yeah who was it?' Still amused with the event.
'It's you isn't it?' she roared in laughter.
'No, it wasn't me,' the girl giggled.
A bang, crash and scream was all that followed. 'Wait a minute, where is Josh?'

Aaron Jhooty (14)
Tettenhall College, Wolverhampton

Trick Or Treat

Halloween. The spookiest fantasy night of the year. Tonight's event was far from fantasy. I walked to Lucy's house. Trick or treating, what fun! Lucy wandered out of the house, her little brother, Will, followed in his white sheet ghost costume. So not scary! At each house, we gathered up our sweets. As the final door closed, I felt a tap on my shoulder.

'Boo!'

'Argh! Oh it's you Will. Stop it, you're not scary.'

Arriving back home Lucy's mum marched down the stairs. 'Why didn't you take Will with you?'

I felt an icy tap on my shoulder...

Charli-Alicia Bloor (11)
Tettenhall College, Wolverhampton

Broken Down

I stood in the cold by my broken-down car. A tow truck stopped, and the driver told me to get in. His name was Paul Brooks, he said. He hooked up my car to his truck and drove me to the garage. When we arrived he opened the door and let me out. I thanked him warmly. Later on that day I switched on the news. The smartly-dressed news reader described a truck crash yesterday. The driver had died instantly. His last wish was to help a young driver in need. The casualty's name was Paul Brooks.

Esa Mahmood Asghar (11)
Tettenhall College, Wolverhampton

WRITING A HORROR STORY

I had no ideas. We were writing a mini saga horror story for a competition. Sighing I sat back and caught a glimpse of my dolls on the shelf by my bed. Perfect! I scribble for ages before getting some water. I reopen my door to see my book at my feet. Bending down to pick it up, I see the words in loopy handwriting 'Come play with us...' I freeze for a second, before rolling my eyes. 'Stop messing with my prep!' I yell down to my sister. Then coming from the shelf by my bed, a high-pitched giggle...

NATASHA EDWARDS (14)
Tettenhall College, Wolverhampton

NEW EYES

It's not nice being blind is it? Well, what would you know? Because you are just really lucky to have decent eyes. After ten years of blindness I was able to see. Thanks to the operation. Since I've had my new eyes something hasn't been right. It could be the side effects but I'm still not sure. At 3.07am I always have the same nightmare. A scream, a screech, a crash and then total darkness. A car accident. It's how she died. The girl who gave me her eyes.

MOLLY DOUGHTY (13)
Tettenhall College, Wolverhampton

The Beast

It was midnight. My phone read 12am. I live outside a dark wood. My cat, Hidey, went missing. It ran out into the middle of the woods, stupid cat. I always go after it. As I ventured out I saw a shaking bush in the distance. I parted the bush and something scratched me. It was just a young fox. As I ventured forward I saw my black cat in the distance. However, something was different. It turned its head towards me and two blood-red eyes turned towards me. I knew this was my end.

Lewis Clarke (15)
Tettenhall College, Wolverhampton

Premonitions

I've been having the same dream constantly; the scary part is I can't tell if it's real. Every night I'm in a war-torn village with the same family. The baby starts crying as the jet approaches, the rumble getting louder. I try to warn them but they can't see or hear me. After the village has been obliterated the father crawls from the rubble, half his face melted away, screaming for his family. Then last night it stopped. Maybe it was a side-effect of my medicine. This morning I turned on the news. 'UK announces air strikes on Syria.'

Zakariyya Ali (14)
Tettenhall College, Wolverhampton

IT'S ME!

I woke up in the middle of the night to the sound of the loud, whistling wind. I turned my head to get back to sleep and caught a glimpse in the corner of my eye - a creepy, torn-up doll on my rocking chair. This, followed by a faint, quick running noise coming from outside my room. *It must have been my little sister,* I thought to myself, as I placed it back in her room. I walked back, thinking it was all fine to find the same doll on my rocking chair again... 'It's me!'

GEORGE SHIPWAY (12)
Tettenhall College, Wolverhampton

TWO FACED

I can't believe Natasha called me two-faced! I move to the mirror and start to get ready for school, trying to do the hairstyle that Mum had taught me. My eye catches a glimpse of a dark figure standing behind me. I spin round but no one is there; I must have been imagining it. Walking over to my bedside table, I pick up my phone and turn and glimpse at the mirror. My face is where I left it, in the mirror, staring...

SIMRAN BAJWA (13)
Tettenhall College, Wolverhampton

Mother

'Hello, Mother is that you?' Darkness consumes the air raid shelter. Shivers ripple through my coiled, frozen spine, as my sister's insipid face stares at the deteriorating portrait. Squinting at Molly, I notice beads of sweat trickling down her face. 'Are you OK?' I ask, but she doesn't reply. 'Don't worry Molly, everything will be all right!'
She's motionless. It's like I'm invisible. 'Lucy, I'm scared,' she whispers.
Phew, she's finally stirred. *Bang!* Wind abruptly gushes in as my mother's quivering figure appears. 'Hello, Mother is that you?'
'Molly, we've found your sister's body; the war has taken her life.'

Orla Shipway (15)
Tettenhall College, Wolverhampton

Come And Play

10th December 2005. Home from another boring day at school. I looked outside my bedroom window to see something that shouldn't be there. A girl in a pink dress, her hair hanging down over her face. I looked back at my bed; I felt a little dizzy. I peeked back out of the window. She wasn't there.
From behind me came a voice. 'Come play with me.' Then laughter. I turned back, feeling dizzy. The voice was coming from inside my wardrobe.
'Come play with me.'
I went in.
10th December 2015 - Local boy still missing ten years on.

Sulayman Aurangzeb (13)
Tettenhall College, Wolverhampton

My Sister!

I was stuck in bed. All the ghost stories we had read in class scared the life out of me. Mum and Dad were asleep. My heart was pounding. I tried to sleep, but my pulse was disturbing me! I could hear my sister on the phone gossiping as usual. I heard a noise! I wanted to go see her but I knew she would kick me out. I plucked up the courage. I opened the door and walked towards her. I tapped her shoulder. Something was wrong. She turned towards me, her eyes flashing green. This wasn't my sister!

Keval Thanki (14)
Tettenhall College, Wolverhampton

Hell In High School

English prep, again here goes. 'The lights flickered on and off and then suddenly blew out.' Finally done. Time to hand it in. I tiptoed my way to the corridor. As I got there, I realised I had forgotten my bag. I turned back and the lights blew out one by one. Just like in my story. I spotted a figure in the distance slowly making its way towards me. I ran for the door. It was locked, just like in my story. Trouble was I knew what I had written next!

Rohan Sharma (13)
Tettenhall College, Wolverhampton

I Hate Maths!

I am looking for my bag after another boring Monday at school. I try in my maths classroom, it's not there, but Mr Smith takes this opportunity to have a rant about my maths test results. I try my English classroom, hang on though, wait, that's weird - it's my maths room. Strange. I try geography, maths again, French, maths again. I race to the sports hall. No, the sports hall isn't there - it's maths. Panicking, I rush to our car. 'Hi Dad,' I say, only to realise it isn't my dad. It is Mr Smith!

Joseph McKaig (13)
Tettenhall College, Wolverhampton

I'm Next!

The light flickered... The curtains moved... Looking for a soul, I heard my brother laughing, 'You got scared!'
'No I didn't,' I cried angrily going back to sleep, peacefully this time. The light flickered again. 'John!' I cried. 'How many times have I...?' I heard a scream outside. I peered through the curtain, it seemed to be nothing. Something caught the corner of my eye. The lights in all the houses were turning off, one by one. Our house is at the end of the street. The lights turned off... A scream, followed by another... I guess I'm next...

Aishah Saeed (12)
Tettenhall College, Wolverhampton

Breath

The footsteps were getting louder behind me, but I didn't look back. Something gripped my ankle and I tripped to the floor. Fear struck my entire being as I scuttered backwards into the corner. My arms flew up to protect my face. I closed my eyes and waited. Silence, broken only by my heavy breathing. I opened my eyes hesitantly and looked around. No one. I continued to my room. I'm so stupid! I always let my imagination get the better of me! I closed the door and sighed in relief. I was safe. The breathing behind me said otherwise...

Tom Farley (15)
Tettenhall College, Wolverhampton

The Red Dress

Someone rang my doorbell again. I rushed to the door. Just managing to catch a glimpse of a dark, red dress waving in the wind. I thought to myself that it was too late in the night to be worrying about this; I had work in the morning. Into a deep sleep I fell. A dream? Everything? My imagination? Surely not! Here I was awake again, realising the whole thing was a dream! I lay back down only to realise that at the foot of my bed was a girl in the red dress, glaring devilishly into my innocent soul! Silence...

Cameron Dosanjh (14)
Tettenhall College, Wolverhampton

Teddy

At seven o'clock each night I snuggle into bed and put Teddy on my bedside table. I wake up at midnight and Teddy's gone. I check in my wardrobe, my table, my bed, even my bin and he's not there. Then, in the morning, he's back. One night Teddy was in the middle of the room, just sitting there. He turned his head to look at me and beckoned me to come and I did. We played together all night. I told Mummy and Daddy in the morning. They rushed up to my room; they haven't come back yet...

William Fletcher-Taylor (13)
Tettenhall College, Wolverhampton

Do You Really Know Your Own Blood?

Just an ordinary day would start with me waking my daughter up for school. But it was different this time round. I didn't wake her up, instead she sat there on the dining table staring ahead at the clock. I was sure that something wasn't right. But Joe reassured me that she may just be going through a hard time as her dog recently died. She left. She never returned home again. I went out for a stroll in the garden; I noticed something, it was a dog, but it wasn't Cody. Within his fur was engraved, 'I'll be back!'

Amrita Clair (15)
Tettenhall College, Wolverhampton

Me, My Dog And It

My house is a converted school. My friends think it's cool, but I hate it. I really despise being home alone, especially at night. One winter's night my parents went out, leaving me alone with Barney, my dog. I went upstairs to my bedroom to watch television, but I wasn't paying much attention. I had a strange feeling that someone was watching me. I turned around to see Barney glaring at me. Phew! The door creaked. I thought it was just my pestering dog, but then I heard a noise, like nails scratching down a blackboard. I froze in fear...

Harriet Tilley (14)
Tettenhall College, Wolverhampton

Stranded

I was driving through a silent, isolated forest when I heard the engine of my car grumble and shut down. I was stranded, in unfamiliar surroundings, with no signal to call. Out of nowhere, an elderly couple appeared. They were doddery but kind; they led me into their small, desolate cottage. They wouldn't sit by the fire - insisting I enjoyed the heat as they told me stories of their lives. When I got home, I searched the couple's address on the Internet, to send a card. Horrified, I discovered the cottage burnt down 25 years ago; everyone inside had died.

Jimmy Hague
Tettenhall College, Wolverhampton

Disappearing Fingers

It was my fourth birthday. My parents bought me a doll with big eyes, ginger hair and seven fingers held up. I didn't understand why. *Ding-dong*. My three friends came rushing in with balloons and birthday bags. I bragged about my beautiful doll. They desperately wanted to see her so they went upstairs. They didn't ever come back down, but my doll was sitting with four fingers up this time. When the police left our house, I hugged my doll. Only three fingers up now. She smiled, 'You're next...'

Priya Tesse (12)
Tettenhall College, Wolverhampton